Beyond the Bosphorus

Geographical essay on Türkiye and Balkans in the recent turbulence

Yasuhiro Suzuki

Beyond the Bosphorus:
Geographical essay on Türkiye and Balkans in the recent turbulence

ISBN: 978-1-64273-275-7

Author: Yasuhiro Suzuki
Project Editor: Yumi Itabashi, Hachidori Inc.
Editor: Andrew Kirkham
Book Design: Lamplighters Label

The back cover photo was provided by PIXTA.

Printed in USA
1 2 3 4 5 6 7 8 9 10

One Peace Books
43-32 22nd Street STE 204 Long Island City New York 11101
www.onepeacebooks.com

CONTENTS

PROLOGUE

The Bosphorus Strait connects the Black Sea and the Sea of Marmara, separating Asia and Europe. Istanbul is located on the European side of the strait, has a vast history, and is home to diverse cultures. In 1988, when I was in my late twenties, I visited Türkiye (Turkey) to investigate active faults and earthquakes with Turkish researchers. In the meantime, I traveled to the Anatolian Plateau and the Mediterranean coast, and was fascinated by the rich culture, the magnificent landscape, and the warm hospitality. After finishing the investigation in Türkiye, I proceeded alone to the Balkan Peninsula and traveled along the River Danube.

Immediately after my solo trip, a revolution occurred on the Balkan Peninsula, the socialist system collapsed, and democratization progressed rapidly. Major earthquakes in Japan and Türkiye occurred in the latter half of the 1990s. Additionally, major social changes ensued. They are the Revolution of Eastern Europe in 1989, the Great Earthquake in Kobe in 1995, the Great Izmit-Kocaeli Earthquake in Türkiye in 1999, the Great East Japan Earthquake in 2011, the attempted coup d'etat of the Turkish military in 2016, and the COVID-19 pandemic in 2020. Hence, the last thirty years around the turn of the century (1989–2020) have been turbulent.

In 1999, the Izmit-Kocaeli earthquake occurred in our former research area. We have been investigating this as we knew there was a large active fault and an earthquake could occur there, but our scientific results were not effective in mitigating the damage. Why did we conduct this research? What did my best friends, Mustafa, Ali, and Şerif, who once researched with me for dozens of days, think after experiencing the great earthquake? I did not have the courage to see the disaster-stricken Türkiye, and I have not visited Türkiye since my second trip in 1992.

Professor Işıkara of the University of Boğaziçi was the most helpful person I met in Türkiye. He always teased me by saying, "Hey, Suzuki. I'll give you a punishment!" However, his eyes were full of kindness. After the 1999 earthquake, he enthusiastically appealed on television that Istanbul might be hit by an earthquake in the near future, and was nicknamed *Deprem Dede* (earthquake grandfather). The TV show was also broadcast in Japan, and I reunited with Professor Işıkara on TV, but unfortunately, he passed away in 2013. I deeply regret having missed the opportunity to express my gratitude to him.

In the fall of 2019, I returned to Istanbul after a gap of about 30 years. At first glance, the cityscape of the ancient city appeared unchanged, but in actuality, there were significant changes. While tracing the memories associated with the place, I caught up with my researcher friends who once worked with me. In retrospect, although unwittingly, this revisit was aptly timed just a few months before the onset of the global COVID-19 pandemic.

This book is a travel diary that examines the thirty turbulent years for humankind, that is only a moment for the ancient city of Istanbul. The introduction describes how I returned to Istanbul. Chapters 1 and 2 are based on the 1988 travelogue on Türkiye and the Balkan Peninsula, "Beyond the Bosphorus—A Sight between Asia and Europe" published in the journal *Geography* by Kokon Shoin from August 1989 to December 1990. Chapter 3 recounts how I walked around Istanbul in 2019, looking back on the turbulence of the last thirty years around the turn of the century and pondering the future friendship between Türkiye and Japan.

As a physical geographer who researches the relationship between nature and humans, I have spent a lot of time during the last thirty years thinking about active faults and earthquake disaster prevention. Active faults are a type of "breath of the earth". Its movements have formed the terrain of the earth over the years, and people have lived on it since. Every time an active fault moves, an earthquake occurs. The ancient city of Istanbul was hit by many major earthquakes and was reconstructed each time. The key to pondering about coexisting with earthquakes may lie in active faults. Türkiye gave me the opportunity to study it seriously.

Traveling around Türkiye, I was fascinated by the exotic climate and culture. After returning to Japan, I was often asked, "What about Türkiye?" And I decided to write an essay to answer it.

Geographical travel essays are not just personal experiences, but are based on the climate and history of the area. They talk about the wind, the scent of the place, the ethnicity, and the human nature of the region, and convey excitement and charm that transcends time and space. The memory of my travels did not fade even after 30 years, and went on to become a lifelong treasure.

Table 1: Eastern European Revolution-related chronology

1985		USSR: "Perestroika" by Gorbachev
1986	Apr.	USSR: Chernobyl nuclear power plant accident
1988	Mar.	USSR: New Beograd Declaration
(1988	Sep.	The author's trip to Balkans introduced in this book)
1989	Jan.	Hungary: Multi-party system
1989	Mar.	USSR: Federal People's Deputy Election
1989	Apr.	Poland: Legalize "solidarity" at a round table
[1989	Mar.	China: Tiananmen Square Incident]
1989	Jun.	Poland: "solidarity" overwhelming victory President Walesa takes office
1989	Aug.	Baltic States: "Human Chain"
1989	Sep.	Poland: "Solidarity" Mazovietsuki administration established
1989	Sep.	Hungary / Austria: Open border
1989	Oct.	East Germany: Honecker General Secretary dismissed
1989	Oct.	Constitution of the Republic of Hungary
1989	Nov.	Germany: Berlin Wall collapse
1989	Nov.	Bulgaria: Peaceful transition of power
1989	Dec.	Czechoslovakia: Velvet Revolution with President Havel
1989	Dec.	Declaration of the end of the Cold War at the Malta Summit by USA and USSR leaders
1989	Dec.	Romania: Romanian Revolution
1989	Dec.	Czechoslovakia: President Havel elected
1990	Oct.	Unification of Germany
1991	Jun.	Collapse of Yugoslavia due to civil war
1991	Dec.	Collapse of USSR, President Yeltsin elected
1992		Bosnia and Herzegovina Conflict
1993	Jan.	Separation of Czech Republic and Slovakia
1993	Nov.	EU inauguration
1994	Dec.	Russia invaded Chechnya
1998	Feb.	Kosovo Conflict (until June 1999)
2000	Mar.	Russia: President Putin elected
2004	May.	Poland, Czech Republic, Slovakia, Hungary, etc. joined the EU
2007	Jan.	Romania and Bulgaria joined the EU

INTRODUCTION:
Time has passed [2019]

(I) The Silk Road route

The Turkish Airlines' TK 91 flight to Istanbul, which took off from the Incheon Airport in South Korea at midnight, flew west over the Silk Road before dawn on September 15, 2019. We could see the word "Urumqi" on the in-flight navigation screen. We are now probably in the sky above the Taklimakan Desert.

This was the first time I visited Türkiye since 1992. I first visited Türkiye in 1988, which was my first overseas trip. The vivid impression of that trip is still inscribed deep in my heart.

In 1988, I took a southbound route from Narita Airport by taking a Singapore Airlines flight. I stopped at Taipei Airport on the way to Türkiye. Before landing at Taipei Airport, there was an announcement made in the flight to not take pictures outside the aircraft. I felt nervous about the security system of a foreign country. As soon as we landed, I saw a palm tree swaying outside the window of the terminal building. Subsequently, I boarded again and arrived at Singapore Changi International Airport a few hours later. After a few hours of transit, I was transferred to a southbound Istanbul flight flying over the Middle East that night.

Four years later, in 1992, I took my second trip to Türkiye. The Turkish Airlines flight I took followed the northbound route. Turkish Airlines started its service in Narita only in 1989. The flight stopped in Moscow for refueling. I was able to see the subarctic forest from the flight headed to Istanbul.

Fig. 1: Temporal transition of my air routes from Japan to Istanbul

I wonder if we could have imagined back then that the routes in the future would be north or south; twenty-seven years later, we are indeed travelling on a straight route (Fig. 1). The aviation situation changed significantly. In the past, we used to think of a map in our minds and imagined the place we were flying to; however, in today's world, the navigation map can easily tell us where we are.

I was also able to feel the passage of time in the "Transit at Incheon." With Japan's aviation administration not making clear decisions, Incheon International Airport has indeed become a splendid hub airport in Eastern Asia, surpassing Narita International Airport and Haneda Airport. From Nagoya, heading to Istanbul via Incheon has become the most convenient route.

Looking back over the past 30 years, I have treasured Türkiye. Although I wanted to visit Türkiye again, I worried about the turbulence. I did not go to Türkiye saying that I did not have the money and time. Since the 1999 earthquake that occurred in our former research area, although I have had the opportunity to investigate the earthquake, to be honest, I have been afraid to visit the disaster area and see the broken-hearted Turkish people. However, if nothing is done, the events of the past 30 years will just be memories. Therefore, I decided to visit and overcome my sentiments.

Right before my departure to Türkiye, Incheon Airport had an exotic atmosphere. The boarding gate of the Turkish Airlines was crowded with Turks. When I got on the plane, I was surrounded by the gentle sound of the Turkish language that has many vowels. The flight attendants of Turkish Airlines wore bright red uniforms and had a friendly smile on their faces. Middle-aged Turkish men board the flight while talking happily with their friends. About 40% of the passengers were Korean and it seemed like there were many tourists. I guess 30% of them were Turkish and 30% of them were from other countries. The passengers were from all over the world, indicating that Incheon has become a global hub. The two flights flew to Türkiye from Incheon at night.

In the business class cabin, the staff wearing white uniforms and hats of a cook were servicing. The meals delivered to our economy class were also lined with Turkish ingredients, namely warm bread, tomatoes, cheese, and olive, despite the flights travelling from South Korea. They have a Mediterranean scent. While the flight attendants' in-flight service was light, the reception was warm.

It takes about 10 hours at night to fly from Incheon to Istanbul. I fell asleep in a comfortable feeling of fatigue. When I woke up, a navigation screen glowed in the dimly lit cabin, indicating that the flight was flying over the Black Sea. The map began to show the names of the places in the Anatolian region of Türkiye, such as Trabzon and Ankara.

Eventually, a map of the Sea of Marmara was projected, displaying the name of Izmit. In 1999, a large earthquake struck this region. Although we were conducting an active fault survey in the surrounding area before the earthquake, I am trying to visit this time there for the first time after the earthquake.

(2) The last 30 years of turbulence

As I approached Türkiye, I remembered various things from the past 30 years. In 1988, I saw the Bosphorus for the first time. It is a famous strait that separates Asia and Europe. Its width is only about one kilometer and the opposite bank can be seen right there. The ethnicity and language were not different on either side, and the researchers at Boğaziçi University, who investigated along with us, commuted across the strait every day by bus.

During my late twenties, I was dispatched as a member of a joint active fault survey team formed by the universities and stayed at the Kandilli Observatory of Boğaziçi University, which is located in a small hill on the Asian side of the strait. I looked down at this strait every day. After preparing for a field survey here for a few days, I went to the Anatolian region with Mustafa, Ali, and other Turkish researchers, and spent a summer there.

After two months of research, I left the research team alone and headed to Bulgaria, Romania, and Hungary on the Balkan Peninsula. Each country has a different language and ethnicity. Bulgaria, Romania, and Hungary consist of Slavs, Latins, and Magyar, respectively. History has recorded various conflicts between countries. Türkiye has invaded Austria as well as the three countries mentioned above in the past. Border control was strict everywhere.

In 1989, the social situation of the Balkan Peninsula changed completely. Following the fall of the Berlin Wall in November 1989, democratization progressed all at once in the Eastern European countries. The Communist Party's monopoly rule was over. Prime Minister Ceausescu was executed during the Romanian Revolution that took place in December 1989. Following the Chernobyl accident of 1986, the destabilization of the area around Türkiye began. The Balkan Peninsula in 1988 was on the eve of revolution.

The end of 20th century was also turbulent for Japan. On January 17, 1995, the peaceful city of Kobe was destroyed by an earthquake of the mag-

Photo 001: Romanian Revolution (Jiji Press, December 24, 1989)

nitude 7.3, which was caused by an active fault beneath the city. Such inland earthquakes have not occurred in Japan since the Fukui earthquake that occurred in 1948. As a researcher of active faults, while I was aware of the fact that active faults have repeatedly caused large earthquakes in history, I was shocked by the damage and tragedy left behind by the 1995 earthquake. It was far beyond my imagination. Following the earthquake, we were able to find out that there were, previously unidentified, active faults beneath the city of Kobe; unfortunately, such post-earthquake studies are of no use to the victims. I felt a strong sense of helplessness and realized that I should not be studying active faults solely for my interest.

On May 28th of this year, a major earthquake of magnitude 7.6 occurred in northern Sakhalin. A field survey was conducted in the month of June. We found an active fault that stretched straight over the ground in the tundra region. We investigated this along with a Russian researcher, which saw we carrying a large backpack and camping for several days. The displacement of the fault was measured amidst the fear that came from sighting the footprints of a bear. On the fault trace, the roots of the tree were torn and had been displaced up to a distance of 8 m. Neftegorsk, a city of oil mining workers near the fault, lost 2,000 of its 3,000 population. The city was off limits and was about to disappear.

On August 17, 1999, an earthquake of the magnitude 7.6 hit Izmit, Kocaeli Province, Türkiye. The epicenter was within our former study area, where approximately 17,000 people died. Although the purpose of our investigation was to predict the occurrence of an earthquake, we could not contribute toward damage mitigation. I had no way of knowing the whereabouts of the boys and girls who gathered with a smile at the time of the investigation and the old men who talked to me at the Çayhane (teahouse) at the entrance of the village.

The social situation in Türkiye has changed significantly since then. In 2007, the president was elected by a referendum. In 2017, the presidential au-

Photo 002: Surrounded by children during an investigation at Iznik (July 1988)

Photo 003: Mustafa (right) and the author (July 1988)

thority was strengthened and a parliamentary cabinet system was abolished. I heard that the situation surrounding national universities was also greatly affected, and that major universities such as Istanbul University were divided into multiple universities.

It is natural for me to wonder as to how Mustafa and Ali are doing. Thirty years ago, we talked about research, society, culture, and life almost every night, sometimes on the street corners of Istanbul, sometimes on the hills overlooking the Bosphorus, and sometimes at the research sites in the Anatolian region. I can recall all of these moments as though they took place just yesterday.

CHAPTER 1

Eternal Türkiye [1988]

Various events around the Balkan Peninsula, such as the Soviet Perestroika that began in 1985, the Chernobyl accident in 1986, the East European Revolution in 1989, the Izmit Kocaeli earthquake in 1999, and the subsequent political changes had a significant influence on the social situation in Türkiye around the end of the 20th century. However, the traditional Turkish culture, climate, and humanity remain unchanged. This chapter is a record of my stay in Türkiye in 1988, when I was still in my late twenties. The atmosphere of the city has remained the same, but the characters have grown older (the titles and ages in the text are those of the time).

1. Encounter with the Bosphorus Strait

(1) Kandilli Observatory

Kandilli Observatory was located on a small hill that overlooked the Bosphorus Strait. A cool and comfortable early summer dawn breeze blew from the strait below. Two hours had passed since my arrival at Istanbul Atatürk Airport. The sound of the cars near the airport, the silhouette of the mosque before dawn, the decrescent moon in the eastern sky, and the silence of this place were all so fantastic, just like the strait below.

I was recruited to visit Türkiye as part of a joint survey by Japan and Türkiye on earthquake prediction. There were a total of eight Japanese members: Associate Professor Yoshimori Honkura (Tokyo Institute of Technology), Professor Junichiro Miyakoshi (Tottori University), Assistant Professor Naoto Oshiman (Nihon University), Masaki Matsushima (Tokyo Institute of Technology), Assistant Professors Yoshihisa Iio and Kinya Nishigami (Kyoto Universuty), Assistant Professor Yasutaka Ikeda and myself (University of Tokyo). With the exception of Associate Professor Honkura and Professor Miyakoshi, six of us arrived at Istanbul Airport on July 1, 1988.

At the airport, we were welcomed by Professor Işıkara from Boğaziçi University. Professors wielded so much influence in Türkiye at the time that we are exempted from baggage checks during the immigration procedure. At this time, the excitement of visiting a foreign country with a different atmosphere began to set in.

We were subsequently taken to the guest house at Kandilli Observatory, which served as our residence until we set out for the field survey. The guest house at the observatory was a quaint building with white walls that faced the strait. The Bosphorus Strait and the bridge over the grasslands were visible from the guesthouse's veranda. As I was admiring this beautiful view, the scent of *çay* (tea) boiling in a pot began to fill the room. Freshly baked bread (*ekmek*), cheese made from sheep's milk, and olives were set on a table for breakfast. The crimson dahlia flowers that were on display at the center of the table sparkled brightly in the white room. Behind the table are Turks with black hair and mustaches. It seemed like a scene from the Italian movie "*I Girasoli* (sunflower)".

After breakfast, we visited the observatory's laboratory, where we were greeted by several Turkish researchers. We met Deputy Director Balamir, Associate Professor Cemil, graduate students Mustafa, Ali, Şerif, Oya, Naz, and Nurcan. Over the next two months, we conducted research together and came to refer to each other by our first names. They were cheerful and kind people who always initiated conversations with "*Merhaba! Nasılsınız?*" (Hey! How are you?).

(2) Scenery along the strait

Kandilli Observatory was located at the top of a hill and was surrounded by grasslands and forests. Premium housing was being developed on the hillside at the time. I was informed that the price of a single-family house was several millions of dollar. Given that the salary of civil servants in Türkiye was about one-fifth to one-tenth of Japanese civil servants, the pricing of such housing was inordinately high. In Türkiye, which was by no means a wealthy nation, only a handful of rich people could afford such housing.

Photo 004: Residential land development around Kandilli Observatory. The Bosphorus No. 2 Bridge can be seen in the distance (July 4, 1988).

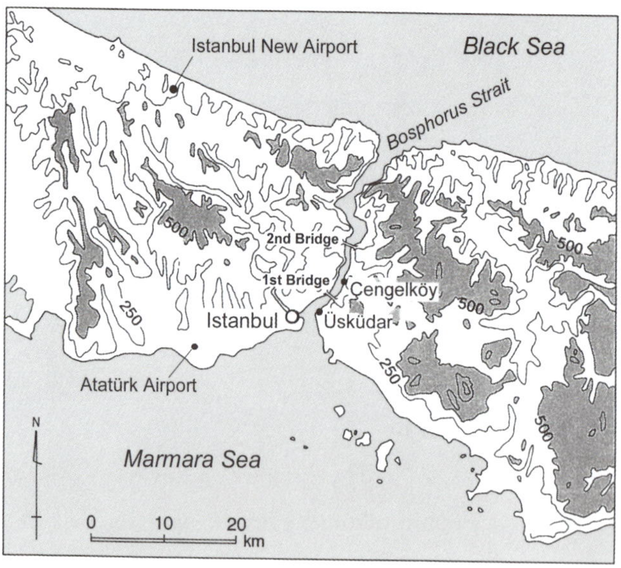

Fig. 2: Map of the area around the Bosphorus Strait (contour line interval: 250 ft = about 76 m) [1988]

The town of Çengelköy was located about twenty minutes down the hill from the observatory. On the Asian side of the Bosphorus, areas along the strait such as Çengelköy and Üsküdar have retained the old housing structures. The strait appeared wider when viewed from the road, which was just above sea level. One could observe large cargo ships and warships passing through the strait frequently, which illustrated its status as an international sea route (Fig. 2).

Photo 005: Warship passing through Bosphorus No. 1 Bridge

Photo 006: Inside the Üsküdar store

Several shops lined the roads. I once went shopping with Ms. Oya in the daytime. I noticed that I was surrounded on all sides by a crowd of Turks. I was enthralled by the sound of Turkish, the various eyes deeply that looked at me with interest, the crowds, and the aroma of the cherries at the fruit shop and meat dishes at the restaurant.

The harbor was at the center of the town. From there, many people would cross the strait to the European side or traverse the Black Sea to the north and to the coastal towns of the Sea of Marmara to the south. Bus routes that crossed the Bosphorus Bridge to enter the European side of Türkiye were also present, but maritime traffic still played an important role due to traffic congestion and the lack of rail routes.

In addition to regular taxis and buses, a nine-seater shared taxi (*dolmuş*) could be used to travel from Çengelköy to other neighboring towns. *Dolmuş* were a low-priced and popular mode of transport. However, since they were not meant for tourists, it was difficult for foreigners to use them. One could get a ride on a *dolmuş* if there were vacant seats, but the fare was never specified as they had no fare meter. When I got on a *dolmuş* with Oya, a woman in a white veil was in the third row of seats with her children. Although the car was old and small for a nine-seater, I enjoyed the carpooling experience. However, I subsequently only traveled by regular taxis due to their relative ease of travel.

In Türkiye, it is rare to see Japanese people outside of Istanbul. As a result, people often called out to us in Çengelköy. Not many people spoke English, and we hardly understood any Turkish, so we typically only communicated with them using gestures. Nevertheless, they were amiable and interacted with us a lot. People generally inquired if we had come there to build a bridge. This was because the Japanese had recently aided Türkiye in the construction of a kilometer long suspension bridge—the Second Bosphorus Bridge. The opening ceremony for the bridge was soon approaching, which had piqued the interest of many locals. The traffic congestion at the time was terrible as there was only one bridge over the Bosphorus. From 6 pm to 9 pm, the bridge was closed to large vehicles. Therefore, the expectations for the Second Bridge were high, and the locals appeared to be grateful for Japan's cooperation and praised its technology.

The Turks' attitude toward Japan were generally very good. They believe that both the Turkish and Japanese belong to ethnic groups that originated in Central Asia. An old man displayed his sense of companionship by saying, "Türkiye and Japan are the western and eastern ends of Asia, respectively." The carefree smiles of the Turks warmed my heart.

(3) *Lokanta* along the strait

A square that faces the strait is located near the wharf in Çengelköy. Next to this square was a *lokanta* (restaurant) that served seafood dishes and had tables outdoors. The Japanese delegation often ate there. The *lokanta's* storefront was lined with fish of various sizes from the Black Sea and the Sea of Marmara.

We did not know the Turkish word for various fish. Dr. Ikeda, who was familiar with fish, would look fish in the aquarium before ordering at the restaurant. The waiters at the *lokanta* remembered us and invited us in often.

Photo 007: Fish food *locanta* (restaurant) in Çengelköy

When we went there during the day, they kindly served us *çay* in small glasses. We always ordered beer there, so they could ask us if we wanted some even if we did not mention it explicitly. The first Turkish phrase I learned was "*Bira istiyorum*" (I want beer). I practiced saying this phrase several times a day.

Photo 008: Japanese member dinner

The sun would set at around 9 pm in the summer. The locals would generally avoid the hot daytime hours and come downtown around sunset. The atmosphere would then resemble that of a village festival. The downtown area would remain busy until late at night. After enjoying some Turkish delicacies and beer, we would buy bread and fruits for breakfast the next day and return back up the hill to the observatory. We often ended up staying in a restaurant for a long time, in which case we could not buy food for breakfast as the bakery would shut.

2. The mystery of the North Anatolian Fault

(1) A joint survey at Iznik.

Before embarking on our expedition, we spent a few days at Boğaziçi University inspecting seismographs, measurements, and other survey instruments that were sent from Japan. It was a fine day in early July. Early in the morning, we loaded our equipment and luggage into the university SUV, boarded two ten-seater minibuses, and left Kandilli Observatory. The team consisted of six Japanese and six Turkish researchers, and the average age of the members was less than 35 years. The target area was around Iznik, approximately 100 km southeast of Istanbul; however, the travel distance was 230km.

Photo 009: Departure from Kandilli Observatory to Iznik

Türkiye is located in the Alpine-Himalayan orogenic belt and is an earthquake-prone nation. Broadly speaking, the earthquakes are caused by the African and Eurasian plates pushing each other. However, the detailed arrangement of plates near Türkiye is complicated. The nation is divided by the North Anatolian Fault into the Eurasian plate in the north and the Anatolian (micro) plate in the middle and south. Since these two plates move in different directions, a shift occurs along their boundary—the North Anatolian Fault—which is where the earthquakes are mainly situated (Fig. 3).

In 1939, seismic activity on the North Anatolian Fault caused a magnitude 8 earthquake in Erzincan, 500 km east of Ankara. A right lateral offset of several meters occurred along the fault at this time. The seismic activity gradually moved to the west after that, and seven magnitude 7 earthquakes have occurred by 1967 (Fig. 4). If one marked the areas where earthquakes occurred after 1939 along the North Anatolian Fault, the western region would remain blank. No major earthquakes had occurred in this region, especially around Iznik, since 1064. Therefore, it was highly likely that an earthquake would occur in this region in the near future.

Photo 010: Scenery of the survey area around Iznik

This region contained cities such as Izmit, a coastal industrial area, and Bursa, which had the fifth largest population in Türkiye. There was no doubt that if an earthquake occurred there, it would cause significant damage. Therefore, several institutions in Türkiye, including Boğaziçi University, would conduct observation surveys to predict potential earthquakes and mitigate any damage. The purpose of our joint research was to investigate

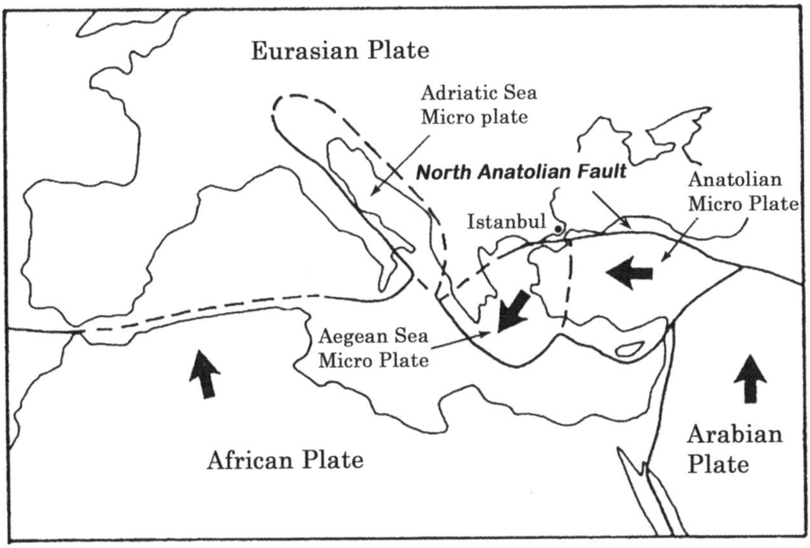

Fig. 3: Plate distribution around the Mediterranean Sea (arrows indicate the direction of relative motion with respect to the Eurasian plate)

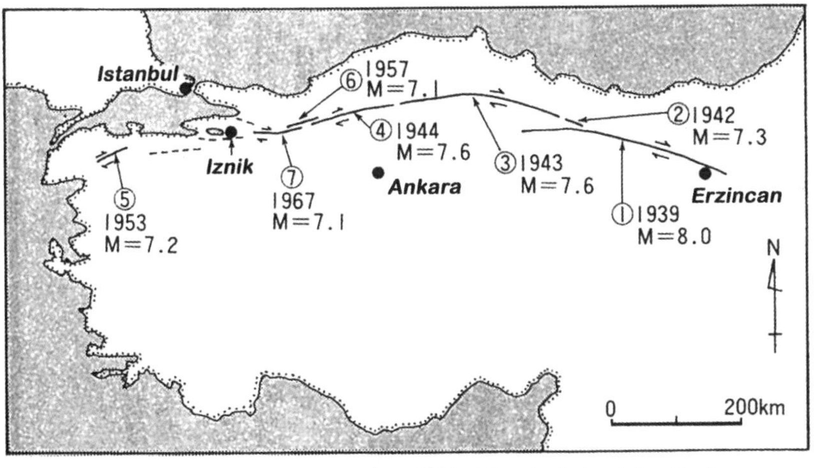

Fig. 4: Large earthquakes before 1988 at the North Anatolian Fault

the mystery of the seismic gap through interdisciplinary field observations.

The seismic observation team installed seismographs in several places and set up an observation network on the North Anatolian Fault. This made it possible to determine the activity of the fault in detail and to follow any changes in it. The geomagnetic observation team captured unique substances along underground faults by measuring geomagnetic turbulence. They attempted to identify precursory signals of an earthquake through such changes in observations. The tectonic geomorphology team located the fault exactly and dug a trench across it to reveal the fault plane. They then clarified the past activity time and interval of fault activity and estimated the possibility of future earthquakes.

We aimed to predict earthquakes in the seismic gap (Iznik and Izmit) by integrating the results obtained by these teams. It was unlikely that a precursory phenomenon would occur during the short survey period, but we sought to contribute to earthquake prediction in Türkiye by identifying the activity of the active fault and the precursory signals that can emerge before an earthquake.

(2) Iznik's lakeside

We arrived at an inn in Iznik in the evening. The sun was still high since it used to set late in the evening. The surface of Lake Iznik could be seen from the windows of the inn (Fig. 5). The inn was a recreational facility for the DSI (Turkish Water Department), which drew fresh water from Lake Iznik. The inn's white walls and light brown bricks presented a harmonious appearance. We conducted the survey over the next two months in the area that spanned 100 km to the east and 40 km to the west.

We consumed dinner and watched the sunset while sitting out on the veranda facing the lake. At first, the researchers from both nations were nervous as we had just met and could barely communicate with one another.

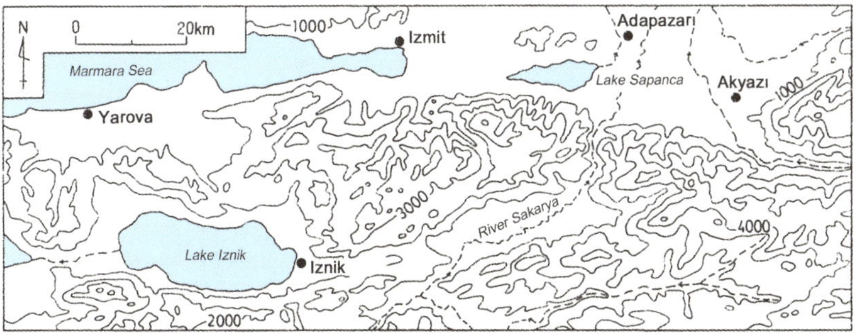

Fig. 5: Topography around the survey area (contour line interval: 1,000 ft = about 300 m)

We were gearing up for the impending investigation to be a hard one. A Japan-Türkiye conflict had already begun within the seismology team over where seismographs should be installed. We relaxed after sunset. As a cool breeze blew from the lake, I consumed a few beers and befriended Ali and Mustafa. We spoke about a variety of topics as the night progressed.

The investigation began the next morning. We met in front of the DSI office next to the inn at 8:30 am. Each team subsequently headed to their respective survey sites. We took along some *ekmek, köfte* (mutton hamburger), cheese, tomatoes, and cucumbers in a plastic bag for lunch.

Photo 011: Japanese survey members gathered in front of an Iznik dormitory (from left: Captain Honkura, Matsushima, Nishigami, author, Ikeda, Oshiman, Iio)

It was cool and dry morning, but the powerful sun eventually began to exert its influence. Each Japanese research team was paired with a Turk so that we could communicate with the locals and taxi drivers. We left the DSI every morning and returned to it by sunset after our daytime investigation. We would then discuss our breakthroughs of the day and think of solutions to problems that occurred. We repeated this procedure for several weeks.

(3) Iznik, the Ancient City

Iznik was surrounded by old walls. There were gates on all of its sides, and roads led into the city from these gates. Iznik radiated the atmosphere of an old town. The roads were nicely paved with cobblestones, but the narrow alleys were dusty. Most of the buildings were rustic and old. The area around the DSI was similar to a European resort town, but there was no such European atmosphere in the city of Iznik.

There was a rotary in the center of the city, and several shops were surrounded it. I was surprised to see a sign that read "Iznik (Nicaea)." This meant that Iznik was once Nicaea—an ancient city that prospered during the Roman and Byzantine eras! The walls of the old buildings reached more than a meter under the soil. Therefore, the entrances of various houses were lower than the ground, and there would be a door several steps down. Perhaps every flood caused sediment to build up and bury these buildings. This indicated that erosion and sedimentation were still very active in Türkiye. This also possibly indicated that the area around Iznik subsided due to crustal movements.

Facing the roundabout in the center of the city, there was an old mosque—Hagia Sophia. The building resembled a Christian church and not a mosque. Its ceiling had already fallen off. According to the board outside the building, the Roman Emperor Constantine had held a religious council there. This council legitimized the Trinity theory and recognized the divinity

Photo 012: The walls surrounding the city of Iznik (about 1.5 m buried in the soil)

Photo 013: Houses in Iznik city. Expanses of farmland outside the walls.

Photo 014: Hagia Sophia in Iznik

of Christ, which later led to Christianity becoming the state religion of the Roman Empire.

The place where such a big historical event occurred still stood after nearly 1700 years. However, it had not been maintained or preserved to encourage tourism. Encountering an ancient building of that ilk was a particularly memorable experience. Next to the building was a non-so-high columnar tower, which a stork was nesting on. Occasionally, the stork would stand up, set its feet, and look down on the street. I felt the urge to ask it how many generations it had lived there for.

3. Field survey in the countryside

(1) SUV ride

Our tectonic geomorphology team joined researchers from the Turkish Mineral Resources Research Institute (MTA)—Erdal Herece and Fuat Şaroğlu. The field survey finally began with a team consisting of five researchers, including Çakır—the driver. The five-seater SUV was a wonderful car that was well over thirty years old. It had a vinyl hooded ceiling and no windows. Under the scorching sun, the temperature inside the car exceeded 50°C.

Photo 015: Interior view of the SUV under investigation

The Turkish roads were relatively well maintained. The paths in the village were dirt roads, but the arterial roads were well paved. Given how frequently the Turks would speed, I wondered whether they believed that all paved roads are highways. I noticed a Mercedes-Benz with a German license plate cruising at a tremendous speed. After tailing the car in front of it briefly, it changed lanes and deftly overtook the other car.

Although our SUV proceeded safely, it was never slow. When it ran at speeds close to 100 km/h, the loud engine noise and violent vibrations would interrupt our conversations. The road appeared straight when seen through the windshield. In some places, we spotted open-air fruit shops that sold cherries, plums, and watermelons. Occasionally, a village lined with clay walls and adobe houses would appear. Every small village had a mosque with a spire. The colors in the landscape were simple and calm. Except for paved roads, the landscape had probably not changed in centennials.

(2) *Çayhanes* in Villages

As the first step of the field investigation, we visited the villages along the active fault and inquired about memories and legends of past earthquakes. In every village, we would first visit the *çayhane* (tea house). It was usually under the biggest tree in the village and consisted of a murky structure with chairs

Photo 016: *Çayhane* under the big tree

and tables lined up on a wooden or concrete floor. The rooms were about 50 square meters in size, not particularly bright, and uncomfortable. As a result, all guests would sit outdoors with their chairs facing the road. Many men would gather here during the day and stay for a long time. No women or young people could be found there. It may have served as a social gathering place for countryside gentlemen.

The *çayhanes* were an important source of information and an oasis for us. I was freed from the heat of the SUV and was revived by the shade and cool breeze. Since foreigners were a rare sight there, we were greeted with a smile by everyone, including the village elders. They regaled us with various stories. We were provided with hot *çay* in a small glass approximately 8 cm high and a some cold cola. The investigation proceeded with Erdal serving as the interpreter.

Photo 017: Interview survey at a *çayhane*

The old gentlemen there knew that we did not understand Turkish, but they still smiled and spoke to us. Although I could not comprehend Turkish, hearing it was calming for me. The cool breeze and calm atmosphere almost compelled me to abandon my research and become a member of the *çayhane*.

(3) Mysterious *Ayran*

More rural villages did not have a *çayhane*, so we would visit the drinking fountains there instead. They would typically be at center of the village. One of the villagers guided us into the village, saying, "I know where the cracks ran during the earthquake." The Turks were kind and always tried to help us. Although their information may not have always been accurate, their desire to cooperate was sincere.

Photo 018: Shepherd boys we met at the drinking fountain

Photo 019: Boys gathering at the *çayhane*

After being guided to various places in the village, we returned to the SUV. However, Çakır—our driver—was nowhere to be seen. Suddenly, a smiling Çakır emerged from a house. The young children of the village followed close behind him. He was holding a large glass bottle filled with *ayran*—a traditional Turkish drink that is made by diluting yogurt with water and salt. The special homemade *ayran* that Çakır retrieved from the house was cold and delicious.

In another village, we were served cold water, fruits, and freshly baked bread. They welcomed us with a smile, even though all we could say was "*Merhaba.*" I was pleasantly surprised by their warm hospitality.

Photo 020: Light meal in the village we visited during the survey period

(4) Convectional rain and pumpkin seeds

On the way back from the survey one day, we encountered rare convectional rainfall as we drove along the Sakarya River. Our conversation was interrupted by the sound of a heavy raindrop hitting the hood of the SUV. Drops of rain began to occasionally penetrate through gaps in the door. The roads became waterlogged, which made vehicles splash water as they passed through. There were times where we could not see anything due to all the splashing water. Nevertheless, I stayed in good spirits.

However, the engine suddenly went quiet and the car stopped. Erdal clicked his tongue and muttered, "Çakır, is it out of gas?" Everyone besides Çakır had no choice but to step outside and push the car. Fortunately, the rain subsided slightly. After pushing the car for some time, we spotted a gas station on the opposite side of the road. We waited till there was a break in oncoming traffic, took a deep breath, and pushed the SUV with all our might into the gas station.

As we sheltered from the rain and looked outdoors at dusk, Erdal bought some pumpkin seeds. We were hungry, so we ate them immediately. They were quite delicious. I was surprised by the rapid pace at which Erdal was eating them. We were then lectured on how to eat pumpkin seeds. We first had to pick the bottom of the seed with our index finger and thumb, and lightly bite the sharp end with our teeth to crack the shell. Next, the contents of the seeds were to be pushed out with force using our fingertips. Despite these instructions, I was unable to improve my pace.

Photo 021: MTA SUV that broke down on a mountain road in the evening. We were able to return because a tractor towed us.

(5) Pious prayer

Çakır was actually a nickname, which meant "blue eyes." The name was too infantile for a middle-aged man, but it was easier for us to remember his nickname as opposed to his real name. He was a cheerful, kind, and devout Muslim man who loved children and often made everyone laugh with his jokes. He would often mutter, "Allah, Allah! Did the Japanese phrase '*ara ara*' originate from it?" Allah is, of course, the Islamic god, but the context in which he muttered that word was similar to that in which the Japanese phrase "*ara ara*" ("oh my!") is used.

Ninety-nine percent of Turks were Muslims. I had heard that Muslims generally do not drink, say prayers several times a day, and often went to mosques. Although I noticed that some Turks drank alcohol and did not pray, there were also some who never drank, always prayed five times a day, and visited the mosque every Friday. Wherever I was in Türkiye, the sound of the adhan would flow from a nearby mosque several times a day.

As a devout Muslim, Çakır sometimes disappeared alone for a short time to do his prayers. One night, he suddenly stopped the car as we were heading toward our Iznik residence. He then left the car, cleansed his hands and feet

Photo 022: Çakır surrounded by children

with water, sat upright facing south, and put his forehead on the ground. At such a time, we would simply wait for him to complete his prayer. Although Çakır would typically have a cheerful demeanor, he would typically grow a bit solemn after praying. The visage of a solemn Çakır in this light resembled that of noble philosopher.

The surrounding area was a plum field. The stars appeared to shine brightly as I looked up at the night sky. I did not pray like Çakır, but when I was near him and sensed the smell of the soil, it felt like a divine experience. I felt like I was surrounded by the land of Türkiye.

4. Living in Türkiye

(1) Daily life

Turkish toilets do not have any toilet paper. Instead, they contain a bucket of water or a tap. The Turks cleanse themselves with water instead of using toilet paper. It is much cleaner than using paper. "When in Rome, do as the Romans do," I thought to myself. Although I wanted to try the Turkish style of cleansing, I did not have the courage to do so. Toilet paper was typically available at various stores, so I would always carry some with me. It was easy for me to use toilet paper in the city, but I had to be careful in the countryside because could not flush the paper there.

Pardon the segue, but Turkish food is extremely delicious. Our breakfast was typically *ekmek*, black olives, and slightly dry cheese made from sheep's milk, along with honey, butter, or jam. *Çay* would always be served as well. "Eating fruits and vegetables for breakfast is bad for digestion," said Vuslat—a college student who aided our research.

(2) Stay at Akyazı Village

In mid-August, Vuslat, Ikeda, and myself spent ten days in Akyazı village, 80 kilometers east of Iznik. We aimed to dig a trench nearby and investigate the active faults. We stayed at the guest house of the forestry office, cooked for ourselves in the morning, and had dinner at the restaurant in the city.

Photo 023: Ikeda (left) and Vuslat (right) placing firewood to warm the bath in Akyazı village

It was our daily routine to brew *çay* in the morning while eating the bread and cheese we bought the night before. Vuslat taught me the Turkish brewing method. We would use a special two-stage kettle to brew çay. First, a small kettle containing only tea leaves was placed on top of a large kettle containing water. Then, the large kettle was heated. Once the water in the lower kettle began to boil, it was added to the upper kettle. More water was then added into the lower kettle, and it was heated again. Once the water boiled again, the *çay* was ready.

By the time we finished breakfast, Cemal—the driver we had hired for those ten days—picked us up in his red taxi. His car has the emblem of the TOFAŞ company, but it resembled a Fiat. We had to travel in his car for approximately 20 minutes to reach the trench site.

A "twisted sickle" is indispensable for shaping the earthen wall in a trench survey. However, we could not find one in Türkiye, so had to go to a blacksmith to forge one. The sharpness and angle of the blade are integral elements, which is why Dr. Ikeda had to make the blacksmith improve it several times before it was finally complete.

Photo 024: Blacksmith in Akyazı Village

Photo 025: Order for a twisted sickle

The trench site was a peaceful countryside location along the Mudurnu River. During the investigation, we hired three local villagers to assist us. The three villagers were friends and came to assist us daily. Their daily allowance was generally 9,000 Turkish lira. In 1988, 9,000 Turkish lira was worth about 9,000 yen (approximately 90 dollar). However, it could be exchanged for only 900 yen (9 dollar) at the bank.

Photo 026: Trench along the Mudurne River fights against spring water

Photo 027: Ikeda (right) and the author (left) observing the wall of the trench, while the laborers, Adem (left) and Hüseyin (right), stare at us from behind.

The trench was 3 m deep and 15 m long, and was dug up using a bulldozer and a power shovel. After the trench was dug, we shaped the walls with the villagers' help. Given that the trench was close to the river, groundwater would spring up from it. Therefore, they monitored and occasionally used a pump-to-drain system to drain the trench. Otherwise, we would drown. The observation period commenced once the shaping work was completed. During this period, they had no particular responsibilities other than draining the water from time to time. However, they were happy to help and we enjoyed having them around, so we asked them to come every day.

One day, I suggested to them that we should have lunch together. They agreed and soon disappeared somewhere. After a while, they returned with approximately 50 river fish. These were freshly caught fish that they had acquired by casting nets on the river. They took firewood from the surrounding forest, ignited it, placed a frying pan on the fire, and melted a block of butter. The fish were lined up on a newspaper and sprinkled with corn flour. Then, they skillfully made a ton of fried fish. It was especially enjoyable to sandwich the fish in bread. Above all, I was pleased with their hospitality. They caught some more fish the next day. This time, we skewered the fish with twigs in the Japanese style, salted the fins, and thrust them around the fire. The salt-grilled fish were well received by the Turks.

Photo 028: Çakır frying river fish

The Turks were often envious of the Japanese because of our high salaries, but I did not agree with

this sentiment. We could often buy some bread at Akyazı for breakfast. One day, we also purchased a big melon. Unlike cantaloupe (muskmelon), this melon did not have a stitch pattern on its surface, and was a little clunky. Nevertheless, it was sweet, fresh, and delicious. The melon cost us only 200 yen. I mentioned that a melon of that size would cost about 100,000 Turkish lira (10,000 yen) in Japan. Cemal's envy turned to sympathy upon hearing that. After that day, they would often try to feed us melon. I lost count of how many times I must have uttered the phrase "*çok güzel kavun!*" (very nice melon). The word for melon in Turkish is "*kavun*," whereas the word for woman is "*kadın*." There were times when *kavun* was misheard as *kadın*, which resulted in some laughs.

Photo 029: Eating watermelon and melon during our lunch break

Photo 030: Village girl

(3) Turkish food and the fascinating *Rakı*.

Supper at the inn usually started around sunset. We typically called for some beer, whereas the Turks preferred *Rakı*. *Rakı* is a distilled liquor made from grapes that is colorless and transparent when it is in a bottle, but immediately becomes cloudy when mixed with water. It is the same liqueur as Ouzo in Greece. Türkiye and Greece were not on good terms, but their taste in liqueur and food were fascinatingly similar. *Rakı* tastes sweet to those who are not accustomed to drinking. The Turks say that it is a healthy liquor that goes well with melons. However, if you drink too much of it, you will easily get drunk. The correct way to drink *Rakı* is to dilute it with cold water.

The supper consisted of a light-tasting *çorba* (soup) with herbs, a salad with green pepper, a *köfte* or beefsteak entree, a pilaf or bread, and fruit. The meal was so light for young people that we had no choice but to supplement our calories with alcohol when we did not eat enough.

Due to the prevalence of Islam in the nation, pork is not used in Turkish food. The most favorite Turkish food for me is simmered vegetables and meat, which was not found in high-class restaurants. These can be fully enjoyed at the popular *lokantas*. I did not really care if the food was oily, perhaps because I was so immersed in Turkish life. I felt a little nostalgic about the similar simple taste of Japanese country dishes.

Turkish has a similar grammar to Japanese, and the object is often at the beginning of the sentence. These similarities are helpful for communicating in Turkish. If you want beer, shout "*bira*" first, then say "*istiyorum*" (I want). If you get lost, shout "*Iznik'e gitmek istiyorum*" (I want to go to Iznik), and the Turks will help you. The trick to speak Turkish is not to pronounce it in English just because it is written in Roman letters, but to pronounce it slowly in the Japanese way. The most important thing is to first look the other person in the eye and say, "I'm speaking in Turkish now."

5. Turkish heart and Atatürk

(I) The Turks' love for dance

The DSI is the Water Department and is a "green warrior" in the semi-arid region of Türkiye. Its various signboards illustrated that it was a fairly large organization. There was a pool next to the DSI inn, and swimming class for elementary school students was held there. One evening after the class ended, a party was held at the DSI for the children. At one point, a sweet 10-year-old girls came up to us and asked us if we would like to dance with them. The Japanese delegation was soon swept up in the whirlpool of dance.

Photo 031: Dance party hosted by swimming class

Iznik is located relatively close to Istanbul, and the girls who were here also had some so-called European features. Nevertheless, their eyes had a certain orientalism to them. Dr. Iio was particularly popular among them, and they would often call out to him. However, it was funny that not only Dr. Iio but also every other Japanese was called "Iio!".

(2) Turkish music

Turkish music has an Asian sound. It is comprised of various genres, but most songs sound similar to Middle Eastern and North African music. The songs consist of several basic types of rhythms with syncopations that are easy to dance to. The tone of a mysterious stringed instrument that produces a sound like an oboe is added to it, as if to invite the listener to dance. However, the tune was in a minor key, which gave them a melancholic feel. The genre of music that Vuslat called "art music" was especially inspirational. The singing voice produced by the straightforward vocalization was full of tremolo passages and similar to *Enka*—a popular Japanese music genre. The Turks greatly enjoyed this kind of music, so it often played on our car stereo.

The Turks are multi-ethnic. Vuslat was of Tatar descent, whereas Oya belonged to the Abaza tribe. Vuslat was a nice man with a tall, gentle face. When he smiled, the corners of his eyes would droop. I heard that this was a facial characteristic of Tatars. Oya was a woman who had brown skin and slightly curly hair. Mustafa and Şerif had black hair with mustaches, Ali had blue eyes and maroon hair, and Naz was a beautiful blonde woman.

Photo 032: Young members (clockwise from the front of the round table: Şerif, Matsushima, Naz, Ali, Oya, author, Mustafa)

One day, we went up to the hills while exploring the countryside. The top of the hill was a vast grassland with a large tree standing on it. Approximately ten children were playing there as they shepherded some grazing sheep. The children's interest was piqued once they noticed us. Oya said something to them, which made them run home and fetch us some cold water.

(3) Barefoot boy on a white horse

A barefoot boy on a white horse followed us. He was observing what we were doing, and he eventually gladly helped us shave the outcrops. I was later told by Oya that the children were Kurdish and did not speak Turkish very well.

Photo 033: A barefoot boy riding a white horse

Photo 034: With Kurdish children. The MTA's Çakır and Erdal are on the left.

Kurds are Arab ethnic minorities who mainly reside in the eastern part of Türkiye and around the border with Iraq. They were often marginalized and in conflict with other ethnic groups. However, they also seemed to live comfortably in many places. On my way back to Iznik, I contemplated on the carefree smiles of the Kurdish children and their plight as an ethnic minority.

(4) Lake side disco

The villa Darka was near the DSI inn. It was a summer resort for rich people who lived in cities such as Istanbul. The atmosphere there resembled that of a European resort. There was a disco inside that would be crowded every night. There were rumors among the young people that beautiful women would gather there, especially on Friday nights.

"Today is Friday," Ali said with a grin. I grinned as well.

We stayed on the DSI balcony and waited for Professor Işıkara, our boss, to return to the room. After the bosses bade us goodnight and left, Mustafa, Ali, Matsushima, Iio, Nishigami, and I snuck out of the DSI. We sought to enjoy a night out.

Oya and Naz—two young female researchers—also joined us on our night out. In Islamic Türkiye, young women are often instructed to not go out into the city alone. Especially in the countryside, it was rare to see young women walking in the city. It was even harder for women to go out in the middle of the night. The only exception was Istanbul, which had a more European atmosphere in comparison to the rest of Türkiye.

The disco was outdoors, near the pool. The cool breeze that blew starkly contrasted the heat of the day. The stars in the night sky and disco's spotlights were in perfect harmony.

(5) Atatürk, the Turkish hero

Türkiye presented a rather pretty picture owing to its beautiful landscape, incredible food, fascinating music, and warm hospitality. However, the reality differed significantly. One day, a man who was casually speaking to me became serious all of a sudden and asked, "Is it possible to go to work in Japan?" I replied, "No. Japan is a small country with a large population, so it is hard for foreigners to find work there." He did not seem convinced by my reply, as he may have found it to be counterintuitive given Japan's significant economic power.

Since the 1970s, many Turks have emigrated to Germany, where they have earned high incomes that they would not be able to secure in their own country. The luxury cars that we would see in Türkiye often seem to belong to such people. In addition, remittances from overseas migrant workers to their home countries are said to be close to $200 billion annually, as of around 1988. In addition, Germany had more than 500,000 migrant workers from Türkiye, and the former was attempting to limit these migrants.

Türkiye's prices were always in flux, and the annual inflation rate was 30% to 40%. When I would send postcards to Japan, the post office staff could never remember the amount I had to pay because the charges often fluctuated. There charges were also different for each post office. Turgut Özal—the Prime Minister of Türkiye at the time—would appear on television daily to discuss Türkiye's financial, diplomatic, and environmental issues.

One night we were invited by Erdal to visit the MTA field camp in Akyazı. It was a five-story building that illustrated the importance of mineral resource research in Türkiye. When I visited, a young staff member said to me, "We are discussing the future of Türkiye twenty years from now. What do you think will happen in Japan twenty years from now?" It was difficult for me to answer this question. Therefore, I did not answer it directly, and said, "Japan now seeks stability, so I don't think there is a need for major changes." They did not appear to understand what I meant.

Until 1938, Türkiye had a hero named Mustafa Kemal Atatürk. Türkiye was defeated in World War I and lost its vast territory during the Ottoman-Turkish era. The land was divided and occupied by Great Britain, Greece, Italy, and France. After that, Atatürk organized the national army and secured Türkiye's independence. He founded the Republic in 1923 and established Ankara as its capital. He introduced various major reforms within a few years of securing independence. He abolished the caliphate and polygamy, banned women from wearing veils, introduced the Western calendar, separated the church and the state, and changed the writing of the national language from Arabic to Roman. He also changed all the names of places in the country to Turkish ones. For example, Constantinople was renamed Istanbul. Tatsuo Takeda's *Türkiye, the State of the New Moon Flag* presents a comprehensive outline of Atatürk's rule. Takeda indicated that Atatürk's aim was to be westernized. Atatürk was inspired by Japan, which succeeded in modernization in the midst of adversity. He also had a portrait of Emperor Meiji of Japan in his room. Thus, the pro-Japanese sentiment among the Turkish may originate from Atatürk.

Photo 035: Mustafa Kemal Atatürk, the first president

The Turks displayed a very strong sense of patriotism. Boys are obligated to conscript, without exception. Ali and Mustafa had deferred their conscription in order to draft their research, but they eventually had to fulfill their obligations (Ali became a soldier later in the fall of 1988). Portraits of Atatürk are ubiquitous in Türkiye. His portrait graces Turkish banknotes and coins, and hangs on the walls of restaurants, bars, and university and government offices. He continues to be deeply respected and loved as a national hero. When discussing the state of Türkiye's politics at the time with me, Ali said, "Every Turk wants Atatürk to return."

6. Trip to the Anatolian Plateau

(1) Two climates

Türkiye is said to have two climates. One is the Mediterranean climate along the Aegean Sea, where Greek civilization was established and Roman and Byzantine culture flourished. The other is the arid inland climate, where ancient civilizations that date back thousands of years flourished. During the summer, our research team split into two and enjoyed each of the two climates.

Türkiye still follows certain Islamic calendar traditions, which involve several annual lunar festivals. The most important of these is the *Kurban Bayramı* (Eid al-Adha: sacrifice festival), which lasts for four days from the 10th of February in the Islamic calendar. Its date on the Roman calendar changes every year. In 1988, the festival was in late July. It is like Christmas in Christian nations, where everyone takes a break from work and spends the day with their families. As was the case with the New Year in Japan, it was a truly sacred day.

As heathens, we decided to go on a trip because we had nothing to do during this period. One night in mid-July, only the Japanese researchers gathered in one room and stood around a map of Türkiye. We were very excited because there was "Japanese *sake*" and "*oden*" in a package that the Istanbul Consulate had given us a few days ago. We decided to go on a trip for three nights and four days. Two potential plans were proposed by Dr. Oshiman, who had visited Türkiye several times and was fondly called "Osman" by the Turks because of how similar it sounded to his name. One plan was to enjoy the azure Aegean Sea, where the midsummer would shine and traces of the glory of ancient Greek and Roman times could be observed. The other was to go inland and see the remnants of the Hittite Empire, Hellenistic or Seljuk Turkish ruins, and the strange rock formations of Cappadocia. The former plan was immediately named the "Aegean Course," whereas the latter was dubbed the "Inland Archeology Course" (Fig. 6).

The group was split almost evenly in terms of their preferred plan, as both plans appeared fascinating. The Aegean Sea group argued that "*Ise ebi*" (Japanese spiny lobster) could be eaten near the Aegean Sea, which would be a fun place to visit as it is a resort area. The group that wanted to go inland made the case for witnessing Türkiye's ancient roots. Subsequently, we decided that we should split into two groups and enjoy both options. I joined the inland team as I was attracted to the plan owing to be lack of knowledge regarding the places in the itinerary.

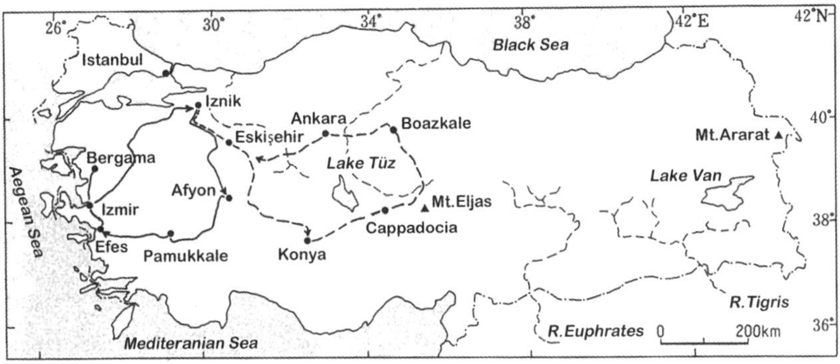

Fig. 6: Two travel routes to experience Türkiye's different climates

(2) Heading inland

We took two minibuses and left Iznik the day before Eid. The driver of the "Inland Archeology Team" was Mr. Recep, who had a mustache and a round face.

Photo 036: In front of two minibuses, before departure

On the south shore of Lake Iznik, there was a mountainous area that extended from east to west. We entered this mountain road and headed in the direction of Eskişehir. As we ascended the winding and sloping road, Iznik appeared to grow smaller. Eventually, we arrived at a pass at an altitude of approximately 700 m. It was the flat, uplifted peneplain that we could always see from the lakeshore.

As we approached the southern slopes of the mountains, the vegetation suddenly became sparse and the breeze grew drier. A sunflower field vividly shone in the sunlight against the blue sky.

As we descended from the mountains into the plains, we came to a small village called Yenişehir. It was a rich rural area with well-equipped irrigation facilities, similar to the area around Iznik. The two buses cruised along a straight road between poplar trees.

The two teams eventually split at the three-way junction. The inland team

Photo 037: Agricultural land on the plateau

Photo 038: Sunflower field along the road

went to the left and the Aegean team went to the right. We prayed for each other's safety while waving to each other's minibuses as we gradually moved further away from one another. The landscape became quite dry once we passed Eskişehir—an old town known for producing sea jewels that are often used for white sculpture. The rolling fields began to spread, and the green trees were limited to the lowlands along the river (Fig. 7).

I saw a restaurant sign on a plain that resembled the Western Americas. We got out of the car and followed after Recep, who led us to a pond full of spring water that some boys were diving into. The water was incredibly clear,

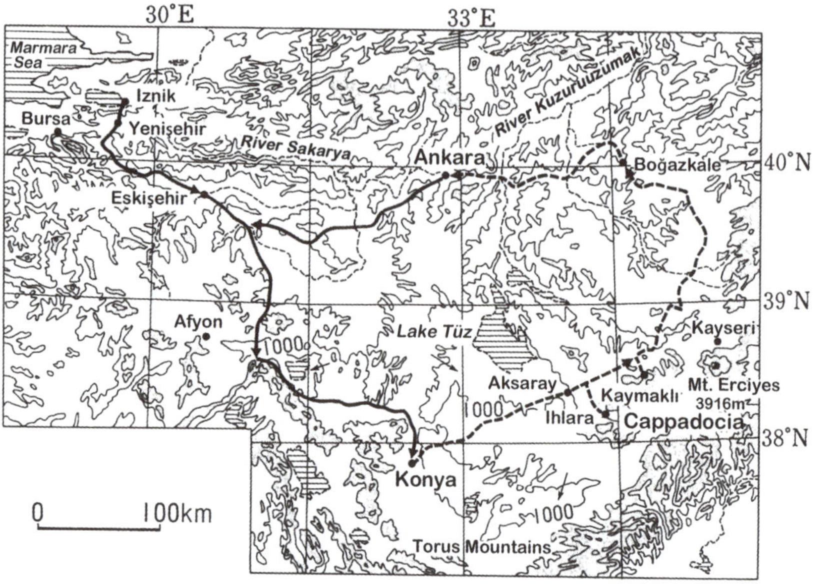

Fig. 7: Inland archeology course

Photo 039: A cool water restaurant. The driver, Recep, is on the left.

and aquatic plants swayed at the bottom of the emerald green. The restaurant was located on the downstream side of the pond and was built on a vigorous river. The pure water flowing under my feet felt cool and comfortable.

The restaurant naturally was had really good seafood dishes. Knowing that we were seafood lovers, Recep had kindly guided us there. However, we wanted to reach inland without being tempted by the seafood dishes we could have enjoyed had we visited the Aegean Sea instead. Therefore, we ordered the same meat dish as Recep. It was a slightly salty grilled mutton dish that was served with colorful vegetables.

After lunch, we set out to reach Konya. The spring area we were resembled an oasis in the dry, barren wilderness. The theme song of the NHK TV program "Silk Road" played on the stereo of the minibus. I remembered that Dr. Oshiman had recommended that we listen to this song as we traversed this region, and I now understood why. We were traveling across the old Silk Road. The poorly colored landscape, the dry breeze, and this blue sky must have not changed much since ancient times. Even more moving to me was the occasional sight of adobe villages. Except for some utility poles and electric wires, I did not see any sights that made me aware of the age we were in. Perhaps there has been no major change since the Silk Road era. The hearts of our crew were transported to the Silk Road era. The theme music continued to play endlessly on the stereo.

A mountain range with a straight foot line was visible ahead. The Landsat satellite imagery brought by Dr. Ikeda revealed that it may be a recently formed mountain range uplifted by the displacement of an active fault. As we drove along the foothills, we saw a well-developed alluvial fan at the foot of the mountain. No clear fault tectonic landform was found, but we observed something interesting.

Several excavated wells were lined up in the direction of the maximum slope of the alluvial fan. It must be a *qanat*—an underground irrigation facility that is widely found in the dry regions of Asia. A horizontal well connecting these vertical wells was probably dug underground, and water must flow through it. Its scale was larger than expected.

There was almost no vegetation on the mountain surface. A horizontal stripe pattern could be seen on the slope of the mountain, and young trees

Photo 040: Boys drawing water from a well

was growing along the stripe. There were many bald mountains in the inland areas of Türkiye. The flocks of sheep grazing everywhere indicated that the vegetation was severely destroyed by grazing sheep over the course of history. Of course, such sparseness was not entirely the fault of grazing sheep. However, a lack of vegetation results in soil erosion, and the mountain consequently completely loses its ability to feed trees. I continued to admire the scenery from the window for a while.

The vehicle almost never stopped and continued to head east. It had been running in semi-arid areas for a long time. Once the sun had already tilted to the west, the city was visible beyond the highway. It was Konya, the capital of the Seljuk Turkish era in the 11th century.

(3) Crowds in the city of Konya

Konya was a vibrant local city with active commercial activities. There were several waves of people in the narrow alleys, and this sight reminded me of the melody of "At the Persian Market." It resembled downtown in Tokyo on New Year's Eve. We encountered in a traffic jam at the roundabout in the center of the city. This was in contrast to the sparse and desolate landscape

Photo 041: Traffic accident in Konya

that we drove through during the day. Although the Turks were polite, their driving manners were similar to (or worse than) the Japanese in the 1970s. I noticed the rotary in the midst of the hustle and bustle.

This is when I heard a destructive sound and sensed a sharp impact. A passenger car coming from behind crashed into our vehicle. This was completely unexpected given that we were completely stationary. The car that hit us was an old passenger car that contained a large family. The damage was not great because it was a rear-end collision in a traffic jam, but the onlookers immediately surrounded us and a settlement with a policeman soon began on the spot.

Although Recep typically did not say much, he proceeded with the negotiations bullishly. We were stationary, so the car that hit us was completely responsible for the accident. After several minutes of negotiation, a compensation of 80,000 Turkish lira was agreed upon. This was a reasonable amount considering the degree of damage, but it was a huge expense for the family in the car behind.

Just as I was thinking that we could finally head to the inn, a man boarded the bus. We started to move and the man guided us downtown. Then, we stopped in front of a wooden door and eventually entered it. It looked like the courtyard of a normal private house, but the man brought a screwdriver and a hammer and eventually started repairing the car. After working on the vehicle for a while, he said, "*Tamam*!" (OK!). The damage had been repaired. I wondered how the repairman was there so conveniently, how much the repair must have cost, and how the money was paid. However, due to the language barrier, I could not ask Recep for additional details.

7. Anatolian climate and ancient ruins

(1) The morning of Eid

We celebrated the morning of the Eid al-Adha in Konya. At around four am, the adhan emanated from a megaphone attached to a pillar next to the hotel. Drs. Ikeda and Iio praised the morning Adhan later. However, I did not know what they were talking about. They laughed when I said that I did not hear anything.

As soon as I went downtown, I realized how special a festival Eid was. Fresh blood could be seen at the entrance to each house. Many lambs had been sold in the market over the past few days and had been sacrificially slaughtered on this day. People hoped to communicate with God through this ritual and gain spiritual stability and happiness. To be honest, I could not help feeling that this practice was cruel. However, I realized that I was being prejudiced in the face of a foreign culture and reminded myself to view the situation with greater understanding.

(2) Horizon and crustal movement

When we left the city of Konya, we noticed a wide field, past which we could see the horizon. The scenery from the car window yesterday displayed a gentle undulation, but this was a completely flat surface. A large salt lake called Lake Tuz, which is over 50 km wide, could be seen. However, this lake was once significantly larger. The white alkaline salts deposited on the surface of the earth and the beautiful lake terraces at the foot of the mountain demonstrated just how large the lake once was. The city of Konya must have once been at the bottom of the lake.

Photo 042: Traces of the former shoreline of Lake Tuz (lake terraces west of Aksaray)

The landscape changed once we passed the city of Aksaray, 150 km east of Konya. A straight mountain range of approximately 80 km in length from northwest to southeast limited the eastern edge of Lake Tuz. The line at the foot of this mountain range (as seen in satellite images) was extremely straight and seemed to have been displaced by an active fault. Besides the vertical displacements that rose on the east side, we could observe a strike-slip fault. There were also many new volcanoes in the area, including Mount Erciyes (Argaeus) , which was approximately 4,000 m above sea level. Relatively small monogenetic volcanoes also appeared one after another on the left and right sides of the bus window as we proceeded further.

We were about 1200 m above sea level, the air was dry, and I felt chilly. Curiously, however, the temperature was over 35°C at this time. The area east of Aksaray was on a plateau-like terrain consisting of ignimbrite (welded tuff) that had erupted from a volcano. Water and wind erosion resulted in the creation of a strange landform on this stratum.

(3) Cappadocia

Eventually, I saw a stream that carved through a plateau. Green trees flourished along the river, and I could see the villagers standing in the shade of the trees. As we proceeded further, we suddenly came upon a landscape that left us speechless. Several tall, sharp, slightly rounded, and conical ignimbrite rocks stood there.

Photo 043: Panorama of Cappadocia (Göreme)

Photo 044: Houses in Cappadocia

The surface of the earth is hard to erode because it consists of solidified hard rocks, but once the valley carves it and the lower erosible ignimbrite is exposed, it can be rapidly eroded to form such a bizarre landform. All of us quickly turned into geomorphologists and wondered how such a landform could be created. We eventually reached the limits of scientific reasoning and decided that it was god's sculpture. This unique reaction of the ignimbrite to erosion was particularly fascinating and would probably excite any professional geomorphologist.

As we reached the head of the valley, we noticed significantly high cliffs on both sides of the valley. This area was named the Valley of Ihlara. If one looked closely, one could find an artificial square hole in the cliff. When I entered one of them, I saw a mural painting inside that depicted Christ. I had heard that many Christians lived in hiding here to escape Islamic persecution. Although some residential holes had collapsed due to slope failures, many of them still remained. Many of the paintings of Christ had their faces intentionally stripped off, and the tragic implications that these paintings depicted were heartbreaking.

Photo 045: Deeply-carved valley of Ihlara

Photo 046: Christ drawn on the ceiling of a cave (at Ihlara)

The remains of human settlements on the ignimbrite plateau were also in Kaymaklı, which I found to be an unbelievable settlement. The surface of the earth looked like a graveyard carved from welded tuff, and it displayed no sense of life. However, below the surface was an underground city where many people lived. Archaeological investigations are still underway, and the full picture regarding this settlement has not yet been revealed. It is a well-known tourist destination, and some of it is open to the public. We noticed a large round stone that appeared to be a door at the entrance of the underground city. It was reminiscent of the life at that time, where the settlers may have needed to be prepared for possible invasions. The underpass was so narrow that I could not get through without bending. There were several big rooms with stiles on both sides of the underpass. It was easy to see that people actually lived down there at one point in time. I was informed that the area was sufficiently ventilated and that tens of thousands of people once lived there.

Photo 047: A large rock rolling at the entrance of the underground city of Kaymaklı

The underpass gradually increased in depth, and its darkness and eeriness scared me. As I began to worry about how much deeper we would go, the tourist passage finally turned uphill, and eventually I could see the light in the distance. It is believed that the place was where Christians resided in hiding, similar to the cliffs of Ihlara.

Göreme is the center of the Cappadocia region. I could see a bizarre cone-shaped or mushroom-shaped erosion landform in distance. I was simply stunned by the scale of the landscape in front of me. It was terrifying to imagine how it would feel to stand there alone at night. A crescent moon floated in the azure sky that filled the background of this incredible mysterious space.

Photo 048: Welded tuff strange rocks and dwelling traces (Göreme)

Photo 049: Mysterious mushroom-shaped rock (Göreme)

(4) Hittite City

On the third day of our trip, we traveled another 300 km through the semi-arid area and visited the ancient Hittite ruins. We approached the south by taking a mountain-crossing route. As I went down the rough road in the desolate mountainous area along the valley, I noticed a narrowed part where the valley carved deeply into the limestone. The towering rocks resembled a natural fort.

The view suddenly widened once we passed through there. We noticed that Hattuşaş, now known as Boğazkale—the capital of the Hittite Empire—was located on the gentle north-facing hillside. We did not see any tourist information boards, which made us think that this old city had just stood there silently over the course of history.

Photo 050: Hattuşaş, the capital of the Hittite Empire, spreads out on a gentle slope (Boğazkale)

According to some archaeological books, the Hittites were the first kingdom to unify the Anatolian region around 1700 BC. The record was detailed using the cuneiform Hittite script. Deciphering the Hittite language in the early 20th century revealed that they belonged to the Indo-European language family and were different from the Turks of the present Ural-Altaic language family.

The Hittite Kingdom fought valiantly against the Kingdom of Egypt in May 1285 BC and signed a peace treaty 16 years later. At that time, the treaty text was left in both Hattuşaş and Thebes, Egypt. Later, the princess of Hittite King Hattušili III became the queen of Egyptian King Ramses II. It is said that Egypt was threatened by the Hittites due to the latter's monopoly over iron refining technology. The price of iron at that time was five times that of gold. The Hittites evolved from the Bronze Age to the Iron Age 500 years ahead of other regions.

Photo 051: Gods carved in the giant rocks of Yazılıkaya, the sacred place of the Hittites (east of Boğazkale)

Photo 052: The Lion Gate in Hattuşaş, the Hittite capital (Boğazkale)

The mountain-crossing road we followed to Hattuşaş coincided with the route taken by the Egyptians over 3,000 years ago. Hattusa's fortifications clearly indicated that the Hittites' eyes faced south. Hattusa had a castle that took advantage of the terrain on the north-facing slope of the mountain, sandwiched between two deeply carved valleys. The entrance to the city was on the north side, and the road to enter the castle proceeded uphill. Going up the road, one would come upon a slightly older "lower town." Marble dwellings and the remains of a large temple could be seen on the left and right sides of the road. Further up the road, there was an "upper town" that was dotted with many temple ruins. Behind it was a mountain ridge, on which walls were built to surround the city.

Photo 053: Walking in Hattuşaş

Upon entering the castle gate, I noticed an approximately 5 m tall and 70 m long underpass that extended to the outside of the castle to the south. The surface sloped gently downhill from there. The cavalry must have run through this gate to go south.

Upon looking down on Hattuşaş from this assault gate, I became aware of its magnificent scale, which somewhat resembled the Greek Acropolis. Although it was not as splendid as the Acropolis, Hattusa's desolate landscape and ancient history were more fascinating to me.

Photo 054: *Yel Cap* (Underpass Gate)

Photo 055: *Yel Cap*, through which the cavalry would have run

(5) Ankara City

Unfortunately, our trip was approaching its end. Iznik was so far from where we were that we decided to stay in Ankara that day. As dusk approached, we reached Ankara—the capital of Türkiye. It was truly a big city. However, it was not as vibrant as usual since most people were indoors celebrating Eid. Recep, our driver could not find the hotel we were planning to stay in, so we wandered around in the minibus.

A police car approached us from behind and urged us to stop. Recep stopped, stepped out of the minibus, and started talking to the policeman.

Recep eventually returned and said that the policeman was from Iznik, and he called out because he recognized us from there. This was serendipitous because we were looking for our hotel. The policeman then safely led us to our hotel. Many ethnic groups have traveled around Anatolia since time immemorial. This has cultivated the Turkish hospitality for travelers, which we were extremely grateful for.

Photo 056: Statue of soldiers in the capital, Ankara

Photo 057: Recep stopped by policemen in the city of Ankara

We were able to experience more historical heritage from different eras around Ankara. Most of the important relics from the country were collected at the Ankara Archaeological Museum, which exhibited beautiful works of art I never thought of as being thousands of years old. All of the ancient works of art excavated from Hattuşaş were exhibited there, and I felt like I was able to witness the world that I envisioned there the previous day. The museum's great exhibits also reminded me that what I had witnessed was just one piece of Anatolia's magnificent history.

(6) After the trip

Our short but meaningful journey eventually came to an end. By the time reached Iznik, the Aegean group had already arrived. Captain Honkura greeted us, and we could see the tanned faces of Matsushima and Nishigami from behind. They said,

"The Aegean Sea was so good. We ate such a big shrimp..."

Although we expected to hear about all the seafood that the Aegean group concerned, we did not offer any retort. I am sure all of us reminisced about the Anatolian Plateau and were simply too emotional to respond. However, I also wanted to someday visit the gorgeous Aegean region or the inland Tigris-Euphrates headwaters.

[Note] Yoji Tatsuta's "The Heritage of Ancient Anatolia" (Kondo Publishing Co., Ltd.) and Yukihiro Omura's "The Empire that Produced Iron: The Excavation of the Hittites" (NHK Books) were referred to in order to elucidate the history of the Hittites.

8. Fascinating Istanbul

(1) West bank of the Bosphorus

In 1988, Istanbul could be accessed from the Asian side of Türkiye through either the sea or a bridge. Lined vessels to Istanbul frequently departed from ports along the Sea of Marmara and the Black Coast, as well as along the Bosphorus Strait. On the way back from Iznik, we boarded from the port of Yalova on the southeastern coast of the Marmara Sea.

When we arrived at Yalova that day, we had some time before our ship would leave the port, so we decided to relax and drink beer at a restaurant on the shore while looking out at the sea. The Sea of Marmara was quiet and calm. As the boarding time approached, the harbor was flooded with passengers. By the time we got on the deck of the ship, there were no vacant seats left. There were guest rooms on the first floor—near the bottom of the ship—and the second floor deck, where the waves were splashing. A wave of people unintentionally pushed us toward the first floor. Except for a few young Europeans with backpacks, all the passengers were Turkish. Eventually, a whistle echoed, and we departed from the harbor. The sunlight reflected off the surface of the Sea of Marmara, and a refreshing breeze blew over the sea. I was fascinated by the hilly Turkish landscape that I observed from the sea.

About half an hour later, a man opened the box he had carried with him and stood up. He gathered everyone's attention and took something out of his box and held it out. I initially guessed that he must be a busker, but I soon realized that he was a mobile merchant. He sold items such as vegetable peelers, fragrant artificial flowers, and idea stationery. After brilliantly demonstrating their usability and convenience, he distributed the goods among the passengers to try. The cabin became lively with the voices of travelers discussing whether to buy an item and children begging

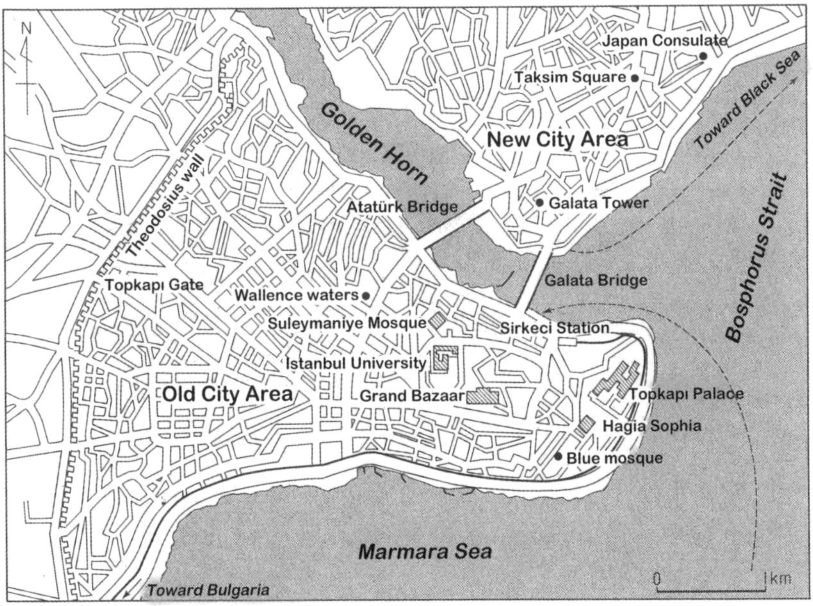

Fig. 8: Istanbul city map [1988]

their parents to buy something. We enjoyed this scene and laughed together. Although we did not know the language itself, we were largely able to follow the events. This entertaining voyage continued for several hours as we sailed past several small islands in the Sea of Marmara. Eventually, the fascinating city of Istanbul came into view.

The harbor was at the entrance to the Golden Horn, which connects to the Bosphorus Strait (Fig. 8). Since the city of Istanbul is on a hill, you can see various cityscapes while you are on board. Three-story buildings with slightly tilted old yellowish walls lined the edge of the water.

The Galata Bridge, which has a pontoon structure, was built in the Golden Horn, and many people and cars came and went on it. The bridge was a little dirty and dusty, but these characteristics gave it a historical feel. It had a two-story structure; the upper part was a road, and the lower part is a promenade where restaurants and tea houses were present.

Photo 058: Istanbul harbor seen from the ship

Photo 059: *Locantas* lined up on the promenade under the Galata Bridge. On the roof is a roadway.

I spotted Topkapı Palace on the hill. It was where the Sultan lived during the Ottoman period, and it had a solid fort that overlooked the strait. A number of huge mosques with dome-shaped roofs stood near the palace, and the minarets (spires) that solidify the four sides of each mosque pierced the sky. While disembarking from the ship, we were caught in a crowd of people. At the water's edge, fishing boats were laid alongside the shore to sell freshly-caught fish such as mackerel, saury, and sea bass. Some men were cooking

Photo 060: Fish markets on boats lined up in the harbor. Men who sell fried mackerel sandwiched between breads.

Photo 061: Yellow cabs and people passing in front of Istanbul harbor

fried fish sandwich on the boat. Small shops selling magazines, music tapes, and sweets lined along the sea coast.

The main street was flooded with many cars. There was a lot of traffic in this area because it was the traffic center of Istanbul, which also had a railway terminal station leading to Europe. It was a one-way road in the direction of the Galata Bridge from the station. Cars ran side by side in all four lanes of the road, and people attempted to quickly traverse through the space. It was almost impossible for an ordinary (overprotective) Japanese person to cross the road. Almost all the confused people on the street were Japanese.

(2) Old Town and New Town

The south bank of the Golden Horn, where we got off the ship, is also known as the Old Town, whereas the north bank is also known as the New Town. Topkapı Palace stood on a hill in the Old Town that overlooked the strait. The Old Town also had Hagia Sophia, which was built by Justinian I—the Emperor of the Byzantine Empire—as the headquarters of the Greek Orthodox Church and was later converted into a mosque during the Ottoman-Turkish period. Hagia Sophia was the number one church in the world for thousands of years after its construction. The Blue Mosque was built by the Ottoman Sultan (Ahmet I) in the 17th century. It was comprised of five main domes, six minarets, and eight secondary domes. A huge stone tower (obelisk) that was brought from Egypt stood in the garden between the two mosques. The traces of the glory of the former great empires were clearly preserved there.

Photo 062: Turkish Islamic Headquarters, Blue Mosque

Istanbul University, which is among the oldest educational institutions in the world, could also be found nearby. Near it was the Grand Bazaar, which was lined with 4,000 small shops that were reminiscent of the world's most proud commercial city. The prosperity of 1,600 years, from the Byzantine Empire to Ottoman Türkiye, was reflected in this lively cultural space.

Although the area north of the bridge was called the New Town, its name only signified its relative novelty in comparison to the ancient Old Town. In the fifth century, Emperor Theodosius II built a defensive fort, which became an important suburb of Constantinople. During the Byzantine Empire, it became an important meeting place for foreign merchants. This tradition still remains. The Galata Tower—a monument to the area that has a cylindrical pointed roof—and the surrounding cityscape have a Southern European atmosphere. There was a Roman-like staircase in the middle of the slope, and old buildings of approximately five stories lined both sides of the street. One could hear the voices of the residents as they walked the streets, and looking up would reveal various pieces of laundry hanging across the alley.

Photo 063: New city of Istanbul, which has prospered since the Middle Ages

A well-maintained park, a hall for international conferences, and a high-rise modern hotel where many foreigners stayed were located near Taksim Square. One could watch European and American TV shows at these hotels. The embassies of foreign nations were in Ankara, but their consulates were in this area of Istanbul. One would see many foreigners walking down the street, and there were various luxury shops that sold carpets, copper crafts, leather fashion, jewelry, and precious metals. Although its political function had diminished owing to the relocation of the capital, Istanbul still served as the gateway to Türkiye.

Photo 064: Copper plate craftsman's workshop

Photo 065: A carpet shop clerk's smile

(3) Asia and Europe in Istanbul

It is said that those who come to Istanbul from the East feel European, whereas those who come from the West feel Asian. The orderly cityscape near Taksim Square and the Southern European building district around Galata Tower certainly made us feel European. Many of the passers-by were blonde Europeans. In the shop windows, one could see sophisticated European fashion interspersed with Turkish colors. The outdoor cafe terrace that faced the street was quite the sight.

Photo 066: At Taksim Square (from left: Mustafa, Iio, Ali, Matsushima)

Photo 067: People of various nationalities gathering at the Grand Bazaar

The cityscape of the New Town certainly made me feel like I was in Europe. In addition, although Hagia Sophia in the Old Town had been converted into a mosque with a dome-shaped roof, the profound and linear structure of the original Christian church could be viewed as a remnant of Roman times. A Roman aqueduct that was built around the 4th century was also present in the city, and there was a huge marble reservoir for water under the ground. This reinforced the notion that Istanbul was a continuation of Europe.

However, except for some foreigners, the people around were mostly Turkish. The sound of the adhan echoing across the city from various mosques reminded me that I was in the Islamic world. Lifestyles and common sense in this city were strongly regulated by Islam. In Istanbul, a woman can walk proudly in the city, which is a rare sight in other parts of Türkiye.

The Turks were tolerant of foreign customs and were reluctant to enforce their traditions upon foreigners. However, they continued to have a strict mindset. In the back of a narrow alley near the Galata Tower, there was an official red light district, which may be viewed as the manifestation of this distortion. A security officer would guard its entrance, and the use of cameras was strictly prohibited. Every country has certain things that are expected to remain and unspoken secret.

Photo 068: Galata Bridge seen from Galata Tower. The new city area is in front of the bridge, and the old city area is on the opposite bank.

According to Shiro Masuda's *What is Europe*, the general definition of Europe in Western history is the tradition of Roman classical culture, Christianity, and the spirit of the Germanic people. Since Istanbul is a city that has continued from Constantinople in the Byzantine Empire, the first two (Roman culture and Christianity) are on display as a remnant of its history. The buildings influence not only the function of a city, but also its image. Thus, the hardware of Istanbul appeared quite European. However, the softness of the locals and their way of thinking was clearly Asian, which is a result of the nation's proximity to West Asia. This is a natural result of the city's history, but when I realized it from the words and actions of my close friends Ali and Mustafa, I felt a greater sense of admiration for their city.

Photo 069: Professor Işıkara and his family living in Istanbul

Photo 070: Author sent off by Professor Işıkara

CHAPTER 2

The Balkan Peninsula on the Eve of the Revolutions of Eastern Europe [1988]

In the summer of 1988, I stayed in Türkiye for two months and then wandered alone on the Balkan Peninsula. I traveled to Bulgaria, Romania, and Hungary, each of which had different languages and ethnicities. This chapter is a travelogue written in the spring of 1989.

The Balkan Peninsula entered a turbulent period called the Revolutions of Eastern Europe after the fall of Communism in 1989. Therefore, this chapter is a valuable record of the place and its people on the eve of the revolution (Fig. 9).

Photo 071: Author leaving for the Balkan Peninsula alone with a backpack after the Turkish survey

Fig. 9: Balkan countries and my travel route [1988]

1. Landing on the Balkan Peninsula

(1) Türkiye-Bulgarian border

"Passport Control"

The low voice of a Turkish official could be heard above me as I awoke in the corridor of a dimly lit passenger car, informing me that I had arrived at Kapıkule, the border between Bulgaria and Türkiye. Since the departure inspection was to be conducted inside the station building, all passengers were urged to go outside. The clock on the station wall showed that it was 2:40 am. As summer was nearing its end, the outside air was somewhat damp and chilly.

A long line of passengers had already formed in the station building under the bright fluorescent lights. There were lively European students on their way home from their summer vacations, Turks and Arabs who were probably going to work in Europe, and other expressionless families whose final destinations I was unsure of. Fortunately, the passport control check procedures for Japanese subjects were relatively loose.

The train on which I had traveled this far was called the Orient Express, an international train departing from Istanbul once a day. However, the

Photo 072: Sirkeci, the first station on the Orient Express

Photo 073: Author before taking the Night Orient Express to Vienna

Photo 074: Railroad from Sirkeci Station to Europe

passenger car I had been assigned was a dingy, quite different from what one might imagine from the name. The night before, upon arriving at Sirkeci Station in Istanbul at 8:20 p.m., 30 minutes before departure, I came to discover that my eight-person compartment was already full.

Ali, a Turkish friend who came to see me off, checked their tickets and pointed to the corridor of the passenger car, saying, "This is your bed." The ticket was double booked and I was the ninth person for an eight-person compartment. This was the reason I was forced to sit in the corridor even though I had a ticket for a reserved seat.

There were various passengers on the train. An old Hungarian gentleman, his daughter, and several Turkish families were sleeping in the compartment I was supposed to be in, and a seemingly tourist-like group of Africans was talking loudly in the next compartment. Since the sleeping car (*couchette*) ran only once a week, the train formation on that day consisted only of coaches.

The train was running from Istanbul to Europe, which presumably would have offered stunning views, but the scenery outside illuminated by the pale moonlight seen from the train window made me feel a little sad. I felt as if I were heading to the farthest land. Bored with the endless monotonous sight of the hills outside, I took a nap for a few hours to rest before the train reached the border.

After a tense passport check, I realized that the Turkish lira I had were useless. I exchanged the remaining banknotes for mineral water at the kiosk in the station. This water and the "CalorieMate" (shortbread-type balanced food block) I brought from Japan were the only food and drink I had to tide me over until tomorrow afternoon. After drinking a sip of water, I lay down again in the train corridor.

When I finally noticed the train squeaking and moving, my watch was pointing at 5 o'clock. It seemed that our train had stopped at Kapıkule for two and a half hours (Fig. 10). Outside the window in the early dawn I could see the Bulgarian-Turkish border, two countries that were known to have a cold relationship. The train slowly crossed the border to Svilengrad, the border station on the Bulgarian side. Here, Bulgarian officers in uniform boarded the train and began an immigration check. The officers were men and women, which was a different sight from Türkiye.

The check on me was brief and far from strict, probably because I already had a Bulgarian tourist visa. However, the checks on the Turks in the compartment were extremely thorough. I knew better than to pry into such a situation, so my gaze naturally turned to outside the window. There were sparse trees, desolate hilly grasslands, and barbed wire.

According to Thomas Cook's timetable, the train was scheduled to depart from Svilengrad at 6 o'clock, but likely due to the fact that the train was at full capacity, it did not start running toward Sofia until 30 minutes later. When I opened the window and looked at the countryside with the cold wind blowing in my face in the early morning, a European woman who was also sleeping in the corridor next to me cried out with an angry face, saying, "Cold." I had no choice but to close the window and look through it instead. Eventually, the relief of being released from the passport check helped me fall asleep.

The rural scenery seen from the train window was peaceful at first glance, with rows of poplar trees, waterways, and fields. However, if you looked closely at the crops in the fields, you would find only a few vegetables, corn, sunflowers, and orchards of stubby apple trees. Much of the land was barren, likely due to it being the dry season. The villages that we occasionally passed by were lined with houses with rustic pale red brick roofs, creating a peaceful and quiet atmosphere. I could see a church-like building, and the dome-shaped roof reminded me of a mosque. I wondered what the situation of Islam was in Bulgaria, where relations with Türkiye were terrible.

The train made its way between less steep mountainous areas and into a wide basin, finally arriving at Sofia, the capital city on the plateau at an altitude of 550 meters, one and a half hours later than planned (Fig. 10). Since there was no in-car announcement that told the station name, I felt restless for two hours before arriving. Fortunately, Sofia Station was big and I knew it at a glance. However, something went wrong here. The train door in front of me didn't open. Other travelers were making noises, insisting to be let off, so I waited patiently, expected it to open. However, the station staff didn't come. Passengers started to board the train through the other

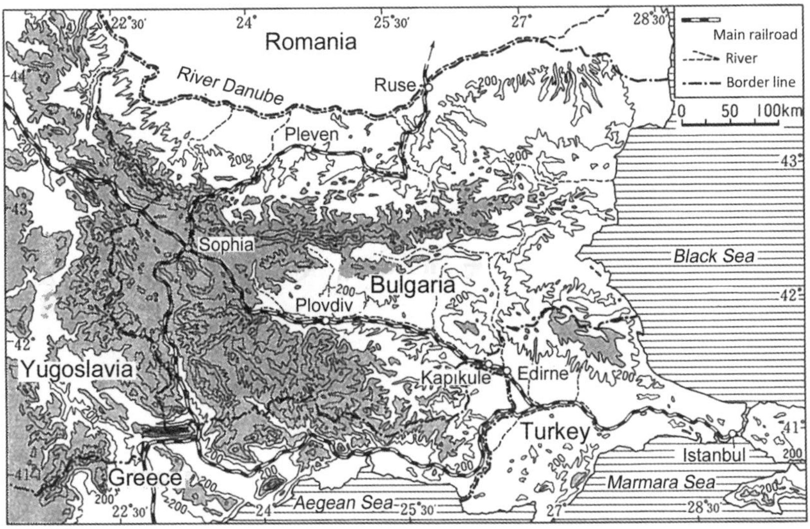

Fig. 10: Map around Bulgaria (shaded over 500 m. Contour line interval: 500 m) [1988]

doors. Finally, I was forced to run to another door, hitting my big backpack against the wall. It seemed to symbolize the difficult journey of reaching Eastern Europe.

(2) The City of Sofia

The Sofia Station building was new, modern, and linear, but somehow inorganic design. The Roman alphabet could not be found anywhere in the station—all the words were in Cyrillic. The fact that I couldn't read the letters may have given me the inorganic impression. When I left the station, the weather was fine, the air was extremely dry, and the scenery looked pale.

The city had a well-developed streetcar network and a well-planned cityscape with many religious buildings in the city center. The Church of St. George was built in Roman times and was also used as a mosque in the 16th century during the Turkish occupation. The Banya Bashi Jamiya Mosque was built by the Turks. The Bulgarian Orthodox Alexander Nevsky Cathedral was built in the 19th century to honor Russian soldiers who died

Photo 075: Cityscape of Sofia, the capital of Bulgaria. The dome of the Alexander Nevsky Church can be seen in the distance on the right.

in the fight against Türkiye for the liberation of Bulgaria. These buildings tell the complex history of the ethnic conflicts that took place here.

In 1988, Bulgaria was said to be the most pro-Soviet country in Eastern Europe. The square in the center of the city featured a statue of Lenin. Bulgaria and the Soviet Union were not only politically close but also culturally similar; the use of the Cyrillic alphabet was one of the similarities. Russian language education was compulsory in Bulgaria, and most people could speak Russian. I heard that the two languages are so similar that if you speak slowly you can understand each language as if you were listening to a dialect of the same language.

There were many restrictions on travelers. Unless you went to the state-owned tourist agency named "Balkan Tourist", you could only book special luxury hotels for foreigners. If you didn't have a bank certificate that you had exchanged for local currency (*leva*) at the official rate, you would get into trouble.

As it was my first experience in a socialist country and meeting the Slavs, the coldness of the female civil servant's response caught me off guard. When I was trying to buy a train ticket at the station and later checking in at the front desk of the hotel, I felt like I was being scolded, but apparently it was

Photo 076: A tram on an orderly Sofia boulevard

Photo 077: Alexander Nevsky Church (PIXTA)

just culture shock and I later realized they weren't actually being hostile. I smiled widely and made a funny face to make the female staff member smile, but it was quite difficult. It may be due to social norms that women's smiles should not be shown to others, as in the Turkish countryside. However, according to my Turkish friend Ali, who grew up in Bulgaria, he could get friendly from a woman by winking at her from the street corner. Recalling that, I was a little confused.

The TV in the hotel room only showed Bulgarian national broadcasts. A show on Bulgarian folk songs fascinated me. The unified voices were like a boys and girls' choir and had a beauty that had been sharpened in harmony. However, because of the feeling of loneliness, the sad sound behind the beauty struck my heart.

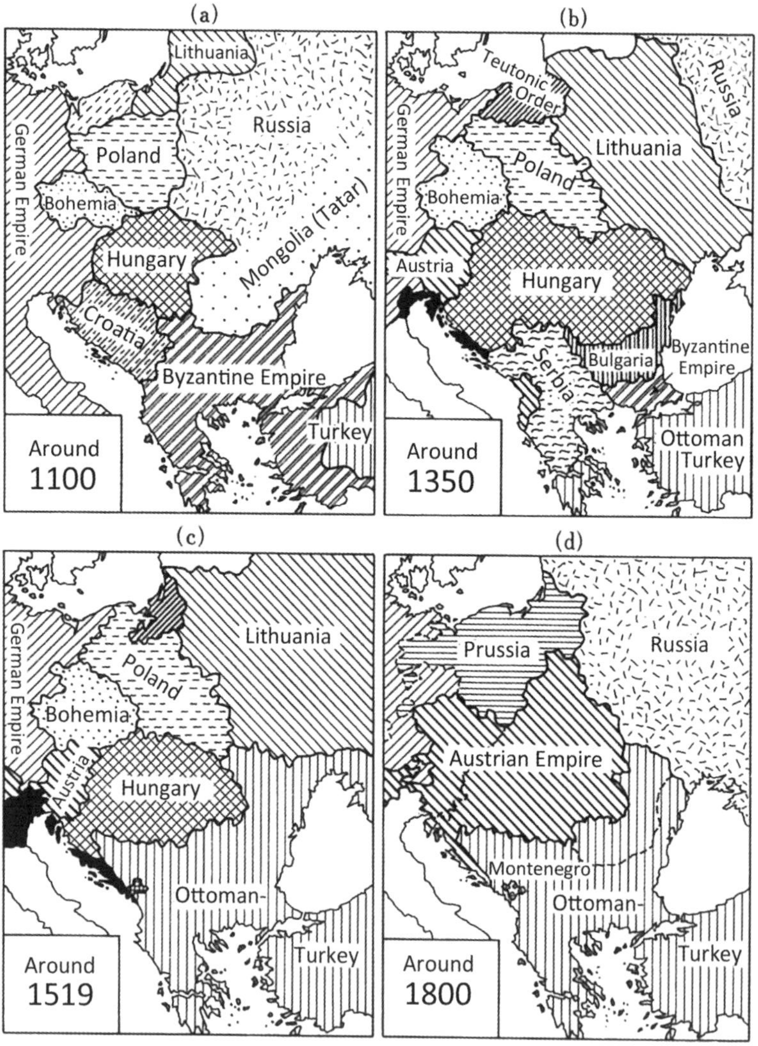

Fig. 11: Historical map of Eastern Europe (N.J.G. Pounds, 1969, "*Eastern Europe*")

Throughout its history, Bulgaria has suffered from numerous international conflicts (Fig. 11). It was ruled by the Turkish Ottoman Empires for 500 years until the end of the 19th century, during which time, the Bulgarian Orthodox Church was culturally oppressed. It was forbidden for the people to pray in their own language. Prior to that, Bulgaria had been under the control of the Byzantine Empire and occupied by the Magyar (Hungarians) and the Crusaders.

Bulgaria is said to have been founded by the Bulgars, an Asian nomadic tribe, in the 7th century. However, after that, they were assimilated into the culture of the indigenous Slavs, lost their own language, and now only retain their name in the country's official nomenclature (Taizo Nakamura, "*Regional Geography of Eastern Europe*" published by Kokon Shoin, and Shingo Minamizuka, "*Ethnicity and Culture in Eastern Europe*" by Sairyusha).

When I was listening to the folk music playing on the TV alone at the hotel, I felt that the various histories of the people of this country were strongly reflected in the music.

Photo 078: Dawn in Sofia. Sofia station can be seen on the left.

(3) Toward Romania

I had some trouble getting on the train from Sofia to Bucharest, the capital of Romania. Sofia Station was not the terminal station type common in Europe at that time. Instead, trains departed in both directions. There were many platforms and the Cyrillic-only information board didn't help me at all. Trains to the Soviet Union as well as Western Europe departed. I had to be very careful to not get on the wrong train.

When I was wandering around at the station, a middle-aged man approached me and said he wanted to buy dollars. He didn't seem to know any English other than "change money," but I showed him the ticket and asked where the platform was with gestures. He said "Okay" and kindly guided me to the train.

I succeeded in getting onto the passenger car to Bucharest and thanked him for his assistance, but he looked dissatisfied and put out his hand. I didn't immediately realize that he was demanding a fee. I understood it after a while, but I didn't feel like giving him a dollar, so I handed over the remaining Bulgarian *leva* bills. He refused these and told me to give him more money. I was annoyed with him. Had the country's economic situation made this Bulgarian man this way? I missed the kind Turks. In any case, I was relieved to move on.

The train from Sofia to Bucharest was almost vacant because it was not the main route of the Orient Express from Istanbul to Vienna. The only other passenger in my compartment was Statis, a Greek student from Athens who was going to meet his brother who was studying at the University of Bucharest. The train, which left Sofia at 8:40 a.m., was headed for the city of Ruse, a border town close to Romania.

It took seven hours from Sofia to reach Ruse. Due to the small number of passengers in the car, a free conductor came into our compartment.

"*Japonez?* (Japanese?)"

Photo 079: Bulgarian conductor and Greek student Statis in the compartment on the way to Bucharest

"*Da*. (Yes.)"

The conductor smiled and asked for a handshake. I was happy because I hadn't seen a smile since I entered Bulgaria. We had a conversation by pointing to a sentence in the Japanese-Bulgarian phrasebook. Eventually, his eyes, following the examples, became serious.

He pointed to a sentence "I want to exchange money" in the phrasebook. Apparently, he was also proposing a black market currency exchange. The black market in Bulgaria offered far more favorable rates for foreigners than official rates. There were two exchange rates: official and non-official. He claimed that his proposal was correct, and no problem, likely because he knew how much foreign currency was worth. It appeared that the Bulgarian people cared about being caught by the police but they didn't think such exchanges were wrong. However, I didn't need Bulgarian currency any more as I was about to leave the country. As soon as he understood this, the conductor suddenly went silent and left the compartment.

Outside the window was a sparse forest area with few tree species. The clear river changed its position from being on the right and appeared again on the left on the track. It was dark black in color, much like the rivers of Canada and Siberia. Occasionally, steep limestone cliffs approached the tracks. The flat land surrounded by these steep cliffs is probably a polje formed by the erosion of limestone. Villages and forests could be seen there. A farmhouse surrounded by well-cared-for orchards and fields came into view. Compared to this pastoral scene, the vast agricultural land surrounding it was harsh in appearance, probably because the exposed limestone and the arid climate were not suitable for agriculture. Gradually, the degree of dryness increased and the grasslands began to spread.

Photo 080: Rural village in a valley featuring limestone carvings

Photo 081: A train traveling through the plains downstream of the River Danuve

The train approached a long downhill slope. The gradual descent to the lowlands and the growing number of trees made me realize that I was approaching the border town of Ruse near the River Danube.

2. The Flow of the River Danube

(1) Border town of Ruse

For the most part, the River Danube serves as the border between Bulgaria and Romania. Soon the train arrived in the city of Ruse, on its southern bank (Fig. 12). My friend Ali, who had come to see me off at Sirkeci Station in Istanbul, was a Bulgarian-born Turk. I remembered that he had said he had grown up in a town near Ruse until he was 17.

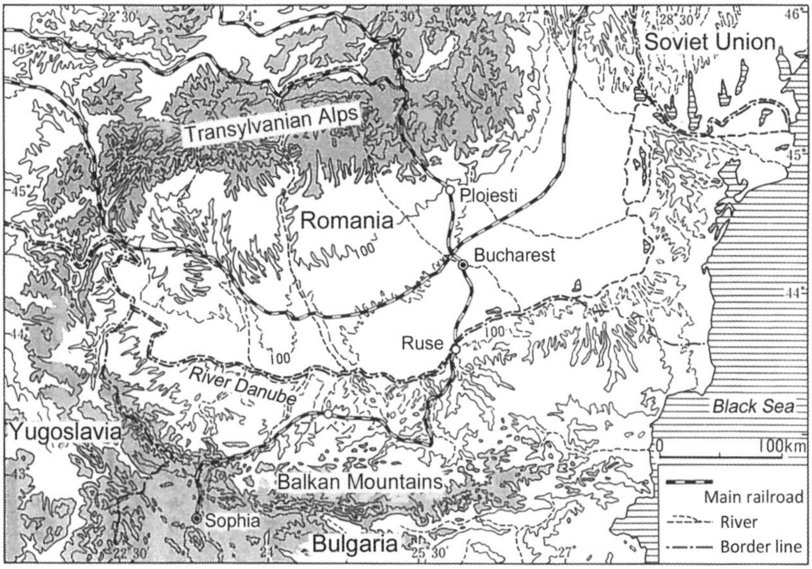

Fig. 12: Map around Romania (shaded over 500 m. Contour line interval: 500 m) [1988]

Bulgaria remained under the control of the Ottoman Empire until about a hundred years ago and is still home to hundreds of thousands of Turks. Although the Ottoman rule was not overwhelming, it was said that during the decline of the end of the empire, the oppression of the Bulgarian people severely impacted people's lives. After independence, of course, there was a reaction and crackdowns on the Turks began. The Bulgarian government enacted strong measures to force the Turks to change their surnames to the Bulgarian style, deprived them of religious freedom and the right to leave the country, and even denied the existence of the Turks themselves. Ali may have been able to leave the country because it was in the late 1970s. I wondered what he must have felt when he first headed for Türkiye from this station of Ruse.

The free Bulgarian kingdom lasted only 38 years (1908–1946), sandwiched between the previous 500 years of Turkish rule and the post-WWII socialist revolution. Kenji Terajima, who described the state of the Bulgarian people in Shingo Minamizuka's "*Ethnicity and Culture in Eastern European*" (Sairyusha), quoted the description of the city of Ruse in the early 20th century by the writer Elias Canetti.

> *At that time, Ruse was inhabited by "people of various pedigrees," including Turks, Spanish, Greeks, Albanians, Armenians, gypsies, Romanians, and Russians. It was not uncommon to hear seven or eight languages a day. Every day, Ruse received a German newspaper from Vienna. Citizens could understand several languages, and the children from villages who spoke only Bulgarian were regarded as idiots.*

This description is interesting because it shows the former vibrancy of the city of Ruse, which was situated on an important trade route, while also illustrating the spirit of the inhabitants. Ali was fluent in five languages: Turkish, Russian, French, Bulgarian, and finally English, which he had begun to study after his arrival in Türkiye. In this way, he continued to reflect Ruse's diversity.

I could see houses, factories, and people planting fruit trees in the fields, giving it the atmosphere of a calm, countryside city. The population was about 200,000, which was almost the same as the city of Okazaki (in the 1970s) where I was born and raised. I felt a much stronger sense of familiarity with Ruse than Sofia and it was a pity that I hadn't planned to stay there.

Since I had come all the way to this country, I should have taken the time to sightsee in cities other than Sofia. Since, as aforementioned, the country has a rather volatile history due to the repeated influx of different ethnic groups, the Bulgarians' unique traditions tend to be more preserved in rural areas. In such places you can find diligent and modest Bulgarians with many family traditions centered on an agricultural base. The home-cooked food there is better than the city food. Sofia is now the capital of the country, but historically it has not always been so. Furthermore, under the post-war socialist government, Bulgaria promoted urbanization at the fastest rate in Eastern Europe, so it is hard to say that the culture and lifestyle of the city are mature. Having come to a socialist country for the first time, I had been quite nervous for the past few days. The meal I ate in Sofia was just to satisfy my hunger. I rushed to the border to escape the tension, but upon leaving the country I found that I still had a great deal of curiosity about Bulgaria.

Looking out the window, I could see a line of houses beside the railroad tracks with persimmon trees planted under the eaves. The sun tilted west, and the long shadows cast by the sunlit fruit trees reminded me that it was the end of summer.

I arrived at the Ruse Station at 3:40 pm, seven hours after leaving Sofia. The train, which had already stopped once, slowly left the platform and stopped again. It seemed that the immigration inspection would be conducted at this juncture. Soldiers with automatic rifles stood before and after the train, watching us.

The first step was the Bulgarian departure inspection. The immigration examination was smooth because it was accompanied by an English interpreter. Then came a Romanian official. All of my luggage was opened and checked, and even the space under the seat cushions was scrutinized. Then a bank official came in and forced me to exchange $10 for each day to be spent in the country into the Romanian currency *ray*. My money was also checked. After counting the few dollar bills in my wallet and shouting "You, problem!" the officer stormed away. Quite understandably, his words made me shocked and worried. It would take another half a day to return to Sofia from here. I also didn't know if I would be able to re-enter Bulgaria because I had already completed the departure procedure. Since I didn't understand what he wanted me to do I had no choice but to stay frozen to the spot. If I walked around, they might find it suspicious. Eventually, another English-speaking officer came and I explained to him that I had a traveler's check. I was extremely relieved when he responded, "No problem."

However, this was not the only problem. When I was asked by the immigration inspector about the length of stay, I answered "Three days." He asked, "Why do you only stay for three days, even though your visa is for ten days?" There was no particular reason for it. What can I say to avoid distrust? Fortunately, because neither he nor I was good at speaking in English, there was no more conversation. Perhaps, as an official, he was just making fun of a young man from a foreign country, or maybe he wanted to encourage me to stay longer. As for me, I was just worried.

(2) Scenery of the lower River Danube

Two hours later, the train finally started to move and we headed toward the border with Romania. Prompted by Statis, who had shared my compartment since Sofia, I looked out the window. Our train was about to cross the River Danube, which was spanned by a long iron bridge. It was the first time I had seen the River Danube. For a moment I thought the river wasn't wide because the train was approaching the grasslands on a sand bar. After that, the train passed numerous small streams before reaching the main bank. The river itself was really wide. A steamer quietly traced the gentle waters, spitting smoke. I wanted to take a picture of the impressive River Danube in the late summer sunset, but realized that since this was the actual Bulgarian-Romania border I shouldn't carelessly point my camera at it.

Photo 082: Large grain field downstream of the River Danuve

After crossing the River Danube, a re-inspection was carried out by Romania, and at 6:10, the train finally chugged toward Bucharest in the sunset.

For a while, it ran over the wide alluvial plain of the vast River Danube, eventually climbing a gentle slope to a hilly area. The alluvial plain, which extended to the horizon, was shining in the setting sun.

Ten hours had passed since I had left Sofia that morning. I was hungry because my lunch had been only one piece of round rye bread and some bottles of mineral water, which were served for breakfast at the hotel. Still, I had some water, so I asked the Greek Statis, who was traveling with me, "Why don't you drink some water?" He rejoiced, "I haven't had a drink since morning!" In return, he gave me a slice of his mom's homemade pizza. This was a big help to me. As we approached the terminal station Bucharest, we shared a small green apple that I had preserved.

Although Bulgaria was an agricultural country, the bread was hard, the apples were green and small, and yogurt was the only delicious food I had found. I had such a low opinion of Bulgaria. However, I realized that the idea of expecting food to be a matter of course was wrong.

At 7:50 pm, near dusk, I finally arrived at the Bucharest North Railway Station. The station was a terminal type and had many platforms. The build-

Photo 083: Greek student Statis and the author

Photo 084: Bucharest North Railway Station

ing and platforms were constructed of sturdy stone and a big clock was ticking on the roof. I wanted to secure lodgings for the night as soon as possible, so I quickly hoisted my backpack and ran through the station yard.

The front of the station was crowded with commuters waiting for buses and trams. In the crowd, there was a bit of a Latin atmosphere, and I was a little excited by the human liveliness that was not present in Sofia.

There was a big park in front of the station. Across the street I could see high-rise public housing and some hotels. I decided to spend my first night in Romania at one of the oldest hotels, built nearly a hundred years ago.

(3) First night in Bucharest

Since Romanians were Latino, I expected them to have a warm Latin atmosphere, but that expectation was disappointing. As this was a socialist country, the female receptionist at the hotel was quite bureaucratic. However, I was relieved to see a man behind her who was charming and playfully pointed to her.

It was close to 9 o'clock when I went down to the restaurant on the first floor of the hotel for dinner. There was no menu on the table. Before I ordered anything, I was served cold chicken and dry bread on a plate. I was thirsty and wanted something to drink. When I asked for a glass of wine, the waiter refused, saying "No." It seemed that he had closed the kitchen because business hours were over. I asked then for a glass of water, but he didn't bring it. I waited for the drink before starting to eat. When he returned, he was confrontational.

"Why don't you eat? You're dangerous. I'll get rid of it."

I was angry, which only made me even thirstier. I didn't think I would get water if I kept silent, so I took out the phrasebook and shouted in a sad voice, "*Dă-mi apă!* (Give me water!)"

For some reason, I succeeded in getting sympathy and finally got a bottle of carbonated mineral water. The water wasn't cold or tasty, but I felt very happy and a sense of hope. It was noisy as the surroundings were cleaned up, but I managed to get a meal that evening.

There were many troubles owing to the tense border crossings and the procedures in socialist countries. Growing up in Japan, a liberal, borderless island nation, I was skeptical of the inefficiencies of a socialist nation. But, I realized that it was owing that I didn't carefully consider the meaning of "border." The "border" was an absolute existence. Sometimes it may be impossible for us to cross it. If the timing was wrong, the person may not be able to survive. It may not always be what you expected. I told myself that I was imprudent to have complains. I lay on my bed, staring at the dim light bulbs on the ceiling. The moment I wondered what would happen tomorrow, I fell asleep.

[Note] Regarding the international relations between Bulgaria and Türkiye, I refer to Taizo Nakamura's "*Regional Geography of Eastern Europe*" published by Kokon Shoin. In 1989, the Bulgarian government sought to improve relations with Türkiye and lifted various restrictions, which were criticized by the Bulgarian people.

3. A Street corner of Bucharest

(1) A Romanian city and its people

I was staying in a room on the fifth floor of the hotel in front of North Railway Station in Bucharest and was awoken by the faint noise of the crowd outside. When I opened the glass windows and broken wooden blinds, I saw a tram running down the street and people waiting for it. It was more like a morning commute in a calm small town rather than a big city. Beyond the street was a park with tall trees, behind which rose high-rise apartment buildings. The people who lived there were coming out to the street.

After having breakfast with *ceai* (tea) and bread in the dining room downstairs, I went out of the hotel. The sunlight was strong, but the wind

Photo 085: Beginning the morning commute at Bucharest North Railway Station Square

Photo 086: The calm cityscape of Bucharest, the capital of Romania

was dry and comfortable. It was about two kilometers to the center of the city, where the Palace of the Republic was located. I felt it safer to walk while checking the map, given that I was in a strange place where I could not understand the local language. I started walking along the main street beside the tram.

There was brilliant greenery such as roadside trees and parks. The road surface was covered with cobblestones and electric lights were hung on the electric wires stretched over the tram. Facing the road, there were old private

Photo 087: Simple private houses in Bucharest

Photo 088:Bucharest University Library

houses and large historic stone buildings. The cityscape was not too modern nor sophisticated, which made me relax.

Naturally because it was a socialist country, there were no advertisements or warm colors in the cityscape. I noticed it for the first time after walking for hours and feeling thirsty. Growing up in a commercial culture, I was not familiar with such a situation of not being able to find a way to quench my thirst. There were, of course, no vending machines. I wondered, "Where are the stores?" My thirst increased and I became anxious. I had seen dozens of people lining up to buy something, but they were not buying drinks.

Photo 089: Passerby in the streets of Bucharest

Eventually, I was lucky to meet a juice seller at a food stall. The juice cost 2 *lei* (about 30 yen at the official rate) and was very delicious.

The city had two centers: One was Victoria Square, where the Communist Party headquarters was located, and the other was the area centered around the Palace of the Republic. Roads radiated out from Victoria Square. Several museums, libraries, large bookstores and record shops, Romanian Orthodox churches, and universities were situated around the Palace of the Republic, surrounded by greenery, thus forming a cultural center. Having heard that some plainclothes policemen patrol the city, I felt little a nervous.

The Republic Museum that I visited had four floors. The first and second floors were lined with works by Romanian painters. There were paintings from the Middle Ages onward, including Christian religious paintings (icons), depictions of the battle with Ottoman Türkiye, works similar to the lonely Munk paintings, and the idyllic but cold-looking rural villages by Nicolae Grigorescu. These depicted Romanian history and climate.

In the second century AD, when Roman emperor Trajan conquered the area and constructed a magnificent bridge over the River Danube, a mixed race of indigenous Dacians and Romans was formed, which is believed to be the origin of the Romanians. This is the reason Romania is the only ethnic group in Eastern Europe that speaks a Latin language while the surrounding countries are mainly Slavic. The area is also said to be a fusion of many cultures because it is on the path of migration from east to west and vice versa.

Photo 090: Painting by Nicolae Grigorescu (1838–1907) (postcard made by the Republic Museum)

The language has also been greatly influenced by other languages. For example, an important word used to indicate "yes" is the Slavic word "*da*." Romanian words for agriculture and livestock often stem from those of the Eastern Nomads and Slavs, and its socio-economic terms include many Hungarian expressions. Romanian ethnic groups account for 88% of the population, but many other ethnic groups, including Hungarians, Germans, and Roma live there. Turkish people live in the Dobruja region on the coast of the Black Sea.

From the 15th century, Romania was dominated by the Ottoman Empire. However, unlike other Balkan countries, Romania was not directly governed by the empire and was given a certain degree of autonomy as the Principality of Wallachia and Transylvania. Therefore, Türkiye's influence in the region was less than that of Bulgaria and Hungary.

Still, during the Ottoman era, the Turks occupied a dominant position, followed by the Greeks. Greek was regarded as a liberal arts language among intellectuals and Greek culture was subsequently introduced. In addition, because it was a key trading point, Jewish merchants played an active role there and influenced the culture. The Greek Church, Athens Palace Concert Hall, and National Jewish Theater still remain.

Photo 091: Romanian Orthodox Church

Paintings of Western European artists, including Renoir, were lined up on the third and fourth floors of the Republic Museum. Surrounded by such richly colored paintings, I felt that this place resembled Western Europe. Before the establishment of the socialist Eastern Europe, there were no barriers other than the physical distance to Western Europe and the cultural distance would have been less than it is now.

(2) A citizen's sigh

I went to an outdoor restaurant in a luxury hotel once in Bucharest. Here I was able to taste Romanian food for the first time. I ordered *salmale* (cabbage rolls) and *chorba* (soup with meatballs), both of which were sour and delicious. Drinking beer in the sunlight shining through the trees made me happy because I hadn't had a decent meal for days. When I was drunk from a strong beer that was 15% alcohol, I started talking in English with a Romanian couple with whom I was sharing a table.

"Your city of Bucharest is beautiful, isn't it?"

"No, development is not well planned and maintenance is inadequate. There are many problems."

They didn't seem to be happy with the status quo of the country. Certainly, the payphones on the street corner were almost all broken and the lamps

Photo 092: A line of cars at a gas station

were dim. I don't think it's good to be over-served and satiated like in Japan, but spending a lot of time to buy daily necessities is never beneficial.

I later found out why the Romanian couple had a clouded complexion. In 1988, the Romanian economy was in serious decline and agricultural products were prioritized for export to repay external debt. The daily bread distribution was limited to 300 grams per person. Unable to withstand such a situation, by 1988, the exodus of Romanians flowing into neighboring Hungary had reached 20,000 to 40,000 people.

The Transylvania region in northwestern Romania was a Hungarian territory until World War I; there have been many conflicts between Romania and Hungary over territorial rights throughout history. Many Hungarian residents still live there. After World War II, with the socialist revolution, the problem of ethnic discrimination temporarily improved. For example, the Magyar Autonomous Region was established in eastern Transylvania and classes were taught in Hungarian at schools. However, the Ceausescu administration abolished the autonomous region, banned the Hungarian names of its inhabitants, and crushed the old villages. As a result, Hungarian residents grew increasingly dissatisfied with the state of society and elected to emigrate. Moreover, not only Hungarians but also Romanians attempted to leave the country. In order to prevent the outflow, a whole family was not allowed to travel abroad together.

It was after I returned to Japan that I learned of this situation. Thereafter, I realized that it was rude to complain that a mere traveler like me was uncomfortable in a country where the people faced such difficulties. Due to the economic circumstances, it was not unreasonable to try to earn foreign currency from foreign tourists. Foreigners were not allowed to stay in ordinary private houses and were obliged to stay in hotels and when they left the country, their payment details at the hotel were strictly checked. Of course, hotel rates were not cheap. Even Category II (intermediate) hotels ran about $60 per night. Credit cards such as visas could be used for payment and there was also a method of paying directly to a bank that exchanged currency or a tourist information center (*ONT*). Perhaps the government was wary of foreign currencies circulating in the market—the rate difference between formal currency exchange and the black market increased more than five times. Hotel waiters and juice sellers often asked, "Change money?" When I asked for the amount to pay at the hotel restaurant in dollars, it was considerably cheaper.

Public dissatisfaction with the Ceausescu socialist government was revealed to the world in the 1989 revolution. In 1988, it was gradually leaked that there was a sense of dissatisfaction with economic and ethnic issues. Under Ceausescu's dictatorship, citizens may not have been able or were too scared to say anything else.

(3) Toward the Hungarian Plain

It takes about 14 hours by express train to travel from Bucharest to Budapest, Hungary. Therefore, it was impossible to complete the entire journey in the daytime. I had to choose which to get through in the daytime, between the two places: the Transylvanian Mountains and *Puszta*, the grasslands of the Hungarian basin. Having settled on *Puszta*, I decided to take a night train from Bucharest. The travel fares were $40 for first class and $25 for second class, which was cheap in terms of Western currency. The procedure to buy a ticket went smoothly and took an hour and a half. I was getting used to lining up first to do anything.

At 9 pm, the North Railway Station was dim and crowded with people waiting for long-distance international trains. There were only Romanians around me, as I stood alone carrying a backpack. Many people had serious expressions as they waited for the time of farewell. It was very different from stations such as Italy, which were filled with tourists. The camera flash was never fired. I waited for the train to enter while enjoying the view of the station at night.

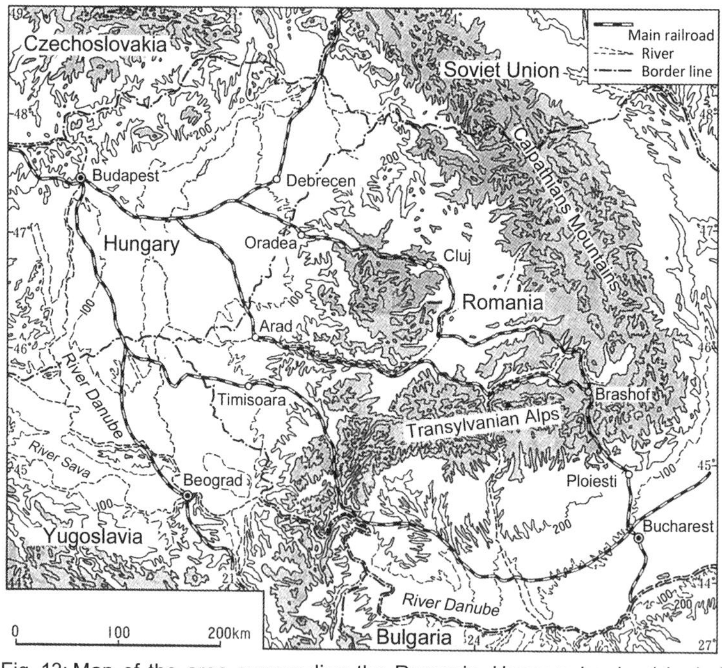

Fig. 13: Map of the area surrounding the Romania–Hungary border (shaded over 500 m. Contour line interval: 500 m) [1988]

There are three routes by train from Bucharest to Budapest (Fig.13). One is a course that goes north from Bucharest into the Transylvania Mountains, turns west in the vicinity of Brasov, and enters Hungary via cities such as Cluj and Oradea. The second heads north but deviates from the first course near Brasov to take a slightly southerly course to Arad along the northern foothills of the Transylvanian Mountains before entering Hungary. The third is a course that goes west immediately from Bucharest and reaches Arad via cities such as Craiova and Timisoara. On the third course, the train runs along the River Danube near the Iron Gate, where the River Danube forms a canyon between the Hungarian and Romanian plains. The other courses are in mountainous areas far from the River Danube. This time I chose the first course; thus, I didn't meet the River Danube again until I arrived in Budapest.

At 10 pm, the train left Bucharest Station on time and immediately left the city area and headed north through the hills. The waning gibbous moon was shining in the hollow of the eastern sky to the right. I saw a quiet village illuminated by the moonlight.

After some time, the air coming in through the window started to smell like oil. At first, I guessed it was because of the smoke emitted by the locomotive, but soon realized that it wasn't as a tall chimney with a gas-burning flame on the top came into view. It was an oil field in Ploiesti.

The train was about to reach the foot of the Transylvanian Mountains. Feeling the cool breeze, I lay down on the bed and quickly fell into a good night's sleep.

For the history and ethnicity of Romania, I refer to Nao Hagiwara's "Romanian Ethnicity and Culture" (edited by Shingo Minamizuka, "*Ethnicity and Culture in Eastern Europe*," published by Sairyusha).

4. A Transylvanian morning

(I) Mountainous area in the morning haze

The mountains from Carpathia to Transylvania are generally said to be the result of Miocene orogeny. However, there is still considerable seismic activity around Ploiesti at the southern foot of the mountain due to the partial reactivation of the old geological structure. This area can be regarded as a crustal orogenic belt that crosses the Black Sea and continues to the Caucasus Mountains. Therefore, earthquake research is active in Romania.

The night train leaving Bucharest was running smoothly through the mountains of Transylvania. The late summer breeze coming in through the window was cool, and at midnight it was cold enough that I needed a blanket, but it didn't interfere with my comfortable sleep. The Transylvanian Alps are a steep mountain range of over 2,500 meters, but unfortunately, I could not confirm what the landscape was like because I passed by them at midnight.

I woke up at 7 o'clock in the cool of early morning just before the sun rose. Because it was daylight saving time, and because this area is far west of the Romanian standard meridian, the sun had not yet risen even at 7

Photo 093: Dawn in the Transylvanian Alps

o'clock. According to the Thomas Cook timetable, I thought the train was somewhere between Cluj and Oradea. It was near the western edge of the Carpathian-Transylvanian Mountains, at an altitude of about 500 meters. The river that runs nearby is part of the water system of the Hungarian basin.

The train steamed through the morning haze along the steep rocks. It received the rising sun on its flank and glowed orange. The surrounding forest was not dense and there was a vast grassland. I saw a farmer in a field watching as his dog slowly chased a flock of sheep. Straw was piled up around a farmhouse, and white smoke rose from the chimney. It was a calm landscape much akin to rural areas in Japan.

Eventually the river widened and the visibility gradually expanded. After crossing an iron bridge, I could see a village surrounded by the morning haze, centered on the spire of the church. The Transylvania region around here was once Hungarian territory, so it is said that there are many Hungarian inhabitants. I wondered whether the church I saw was Romanian Orthodox or mainstream Hungarian Catholic. If the church was a mosque, the landscape would have resembled Türkiye, which I was accustomed to during the summer.

Photo 094: Rural village in the Transylvania

Photo 095: Marshalling yard near Oradea, Romania

The train shot out on to the plains. There was a large field with piles of straw and several farmers holding sickles with long handles and bow-shaped blades gathered to do farm work. At 8:30, in the bright morning sun, the train had almost reached Oradea, a small city with a population of about 100,000 situated on the eastern edge of the Hungarian basin with the border between Romania and Hungary just around the corner. The train began to slow down. When I opened the window wide and leaned forward to look out, the refreshing breeze of the morning blew into the compartment.

A tall church towered above the cityscape. I saw a new church with a spire with a triangular roof and an old church with a cross on a dome. I could also see the marshalling yard. The few passenger cars lined up there were all dark in color and looked old. The letters on the flanks of the trains were Cyrillic, indicating that those cars were from the Soviet Union.

About 10 minutes after leaving the city of Oradea, the train finally arrived at the border station, Episcopia. My relaxed mood disappeared, knowing that passport control was to commence again.

(2) The Romania-Hungary border

In the first part of the Romanian immigration inspection an official came in, looked at my passport, checked the length of my stay in Romania, and filled out the hotel payment details and the official redemption certificate on the back of the departure card. If there had been any discrepancies between these, I would have been in serious trouble. However, in Bucharest, I was confident that I did not go on any strange adventures and followed the rules to a tee to avoid trouble. Even so, I couldn't help but observe the officer's facial expressions.

"OK," said the official.

I was relieved when I got the departure stamp on my passport. I had passed the first step.

Next came a female officer. It was time to check the luggage. In addition to going through my backpack, she also examined the accessory case for my passport. Then a dog came in with an officer. When the dog suddenly approached my knees, I was nervous and stiff. If I didn't like dogs, I would have screamed and that would have been bad. Fortunately, I love dogs, so I could enjoy the situation. The first one to come was a shepherd dog. With a wise and fearless face, he faithfully performed his duties and used his nose

Photo 096: Guards and investigative dogs at Episcopia Station on the Romania–Hungary border

to sniff my backpack. He didn't sense any anomalies, so he quickly turned around and left, just like an official in a socialist country. After he left, a medium-sized dog with slightly longer black and white hair came next. Observing the next officer's serious appearance and gestures, I just smiled. Did the two dogs come with different missions? After completing his mission, the second dog also went out of the car and left with the officer. I inadvertently pointed the camera at its back. At that moment, the guard looked at me and blew his whistle.

"Oops!"

Just then, the train started moving slowly. Fortunately, there seemed to be no sign that a guard with a gun would jump on the train.

Border guards were probably watching over us with binoculars from the tall lookout huts scattered around. However, there was a peaceful rural landscape that made me forget about them. A farmer heading for work was driving his truck slowly along the road. However, even in such a seemingly calm place, there was no doubt that it was a tense border area for both Romania and Hungary.

After crossing the border, the train stopped again. The next immigration point on the Hungarian side was relatively easier and took all of 30 minutes. Hungary had an open attitude toward Western countries, while still maintaining a policy that was in line with the Soviet Union. Therefore, it probably did not strictly check tourists from Japan, which is considered a member of Western countries. In contrast, the checks on Romanians were very strict.

(3) Passing through *Puszta* to Budapest

After crossing the border, I turned my watch back an hour. It was the first time difference I had experienced since I had left Türkiye. It's interesting that even though the length of my experience was the same, I felt like I had gained an extra hour.

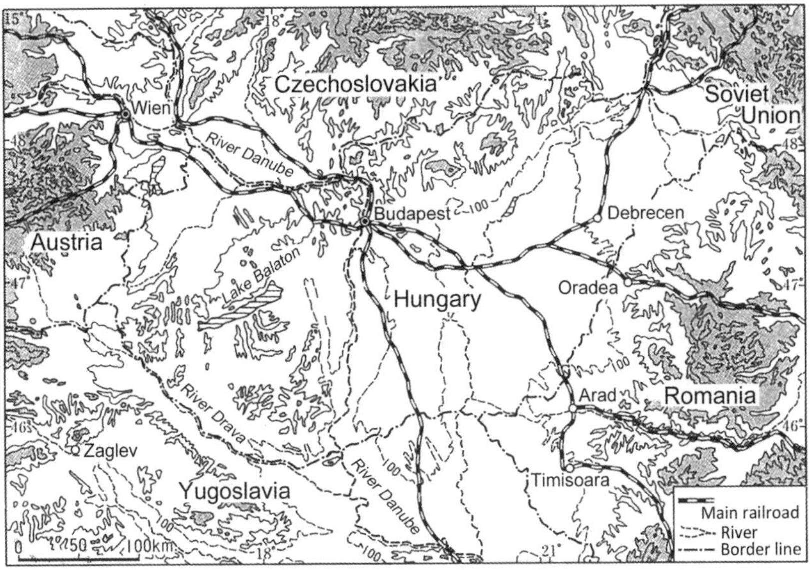

Fig. 14: Map of Hungary (shaded over 500 m. Contour line interval: 500 m) [1988]

I heard that *Puszta*, the Great Plain of Hungary, was a large agricultural area known as the "Granary of Eastern Europe." However, the scale was far beyond what I had imagined. The endless expanse of cultivated land was surrounded by well-arranged waterways and was divided into corn fields and wheat fields by lines of trees. The crops had been planted in straight rows and a large combine was working the field, which was something I had never seen in Japan. I was surprised by the size and abundance of the Hungarian farmland as the farmlands of Bulgaria and Romania, as seen from the train window, were not very rich. This was the rich land of Hungary, which a former Ottoman Sultan had also admired (Fig. 14).

I finally slipped into Budapest West Station at 12:30 Hungarian time. The cityscape of Budapest, which had begun to appear a while ago, was colorful and beautifully arranged. I saw a Catholic cathedral and a young woman in fine clothes crossing the road. I had never expected to see such

Photo 097: Largescale farm on the Hungarian Plain (*Puszta*)

Photo 098: Catholic church near Budapest

luxury and brightness on this trip; nevertheless, the scenery brightened my mood because I hadn't seen such views for some days.

There were two railway stations in Budapest. Trains to Vienna via Budapest enter the East Station and trains to Prague or Berlin via Budapest enter the West Station. The final destination of the train I got on was Berlin, so I arrived at the West Station. The luxury of the station building was inferior to that of the East Station, but the West Station, which was covered with a large triangular roof, was still glass-walled and bright. The information at the station was easy to understand because it was well-arranged for tourists.

When I got out of the station building, a taxi driver casually called out to me.

"Hey, I know a good cheap hotel!"

It was a tourist-friendly invitation that I hadn't heard for days. It was fun to feel the expectation that something might be interesting. But this time, unfortunately, such curiosity was suppressed by a feeling of fatigue. I did not confirm the truth of the invitation, but told the driver instead the name of the hotel on the banks of the River Danube that I planned to stay at.

5. Reaching the country of the Magyar

(1) Reunion with the River Danube

From the windows of the taxi from the Budapest West Station, I could see the huge neo-Gothic Parliament Building, spacious artistic gardens, large rows of broad-leaved trees, and magnificent buildings. I was fascinated by the scenery and let out a sigh. Then the field of view suddenly expanded. That was because the taxi had arrived at the banks of the River Danube. I was reunited with the River Danube for the first time in a long time since nervously looking at it from the iron bridge on the border between Bulgaria and Romania.

Photo 099: Crossing the Chain Bridge to Buda Hill

The River Danube flows through Austria and then eastward along the Czechoslovakia-Hungary border. Once in Hungary, it crosses the hills on the western edge of the Hungarian basin and turns southward. The city of Budapest is located on the eastern edge of the hills. The hilly area on the west side of the river is called "Buda" and the downtown on the east side is called "Pest." Once separate, the two cities were connected by the Chain Bridge in the 19th century to become "Budapest."

Currently, there are eight bridges on the River Danube in Budapest. Of these, the Chain Bridge is not only historically important but also stands out as having a symbolic presence. Standing at the foot of the Chain Bridge, I was amazed by its majesty. Two giant lion statues sit on the thick stone piers on both sides of the river, which are several tens of meters high. Looking up while crossing the bridge, it seems as if we are going through the *Arc de Triomphe*.

(2) The Hill of Buda

On the west side of the Chain Bridge was the city of Buda (Fig. 15). Along the river, there was a boat-shaped isolated hill, on the southern half of which was the gorgeous former Hungarian Royal Palace, a large white citadel with a green-blue dome roof in the center. Looking up from the foot of the hill, its magnificent appearance could not be properly captured by the camera lens.

On the northern half of the hill was a town with several churches. From the banks of the River Danube, we can walk up there. There was a peaceful slope surrounded by trees. From the middle of the slope, the gently curving River Danube, Margaret Island on a sandbar, and the city of Pest on the opposite bank could be seen shining in the bright sunlight. In addition, the Parliament Building, which was built during the Austro-Hungarian Empire in the 19th century, was reflected on the surface of the river. It was a beautiful landscape of the riverbank that could be praised as the "Queen of Danube."

A building called "Fisherman's Fort" is perched menacingly on the edge of the hill. This fort has a corridor-shaped wall that was once built for defense. It is made of pure white stone and has a lookout with a neo-Romanesque conical

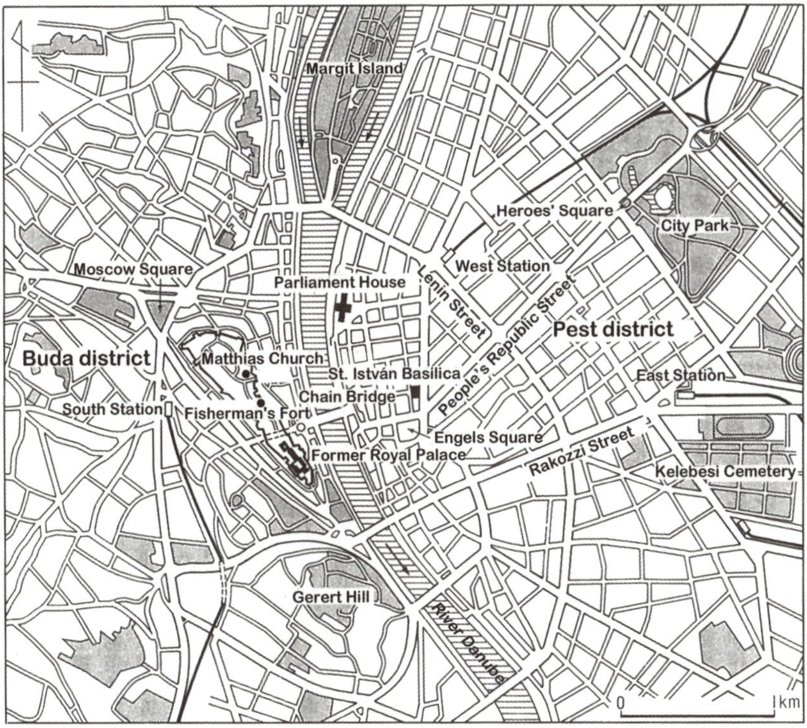

Fig. 15: Budapest city map [1988]

Photo 100: The elegant Hungarian Parliament Building on the other side of the River Danube

Photo 101: Fisherman's Fort and a statue of King Magyar

Photo 102: River Danube and Chain Bridge seen from Buda Hill. The opposite bank is the city of Pest.

roof. It was designed to have a soft curve, reminiscent of the world of fairy tales. Looking at it, it's hard to believe this was a battle wall. While observing the beautiful marble fort, I became keenly aware of the peaceful ambiance of this country. Due to being a lookout, of course, the corridor above the fort had a superb view of the river Danube and the city of Pest.

At the back of the fort was a church with a spire that was nearly 100 meters high. This church, called Matthias Church, was built in the 13th century and was also the venue for the coronation of successive Hungarian kings. However, during the 16th and 18th centuries, the country was occupied by Türkiye. At that time, it was used as a mosque where the Quran was sung. How did the Quran's verses from a Gothic church with a linear design, so unlike a Turkish-style dome mosque, echo over the River Danube?

Photo 103: Matthias Church, site of the coronation of successive Hungarian kings

There were other historic wars. During World War II, German and Soviet troops set up positions in Buda and Pest, respectively. The bullet marks made then still remain on some buildings as painful minders of that time.

Under the fort, a large hardwood tree that had begun to turn red was swaying in the gentle early autumn breeze. How much of the history of Budapest had this tree seen?

Looking back at the inside of the fort, an equestrian statue of Stephen I, the first king of Hungary, stood between the fort and the church. The pedestal was engraved with the story of Hungarian prosperity since the 9th century as a relief, showing off the tradition of the nomadic Magyar from Asia.

The area of Buda Hill was a very quiet place. The colors of the walls of the building were unified in pale yellow, white, brick, dark brown, and so on, and it was beautifully harmonized with the roof of the church decorated with bright tiles of similar colors and topped by a pure white spire.

There was also a Bartok Memorial in that area. Bartok's music has a profound and solemn sound. It gives an image of anxiety that is felt when confronting a huge object. I thought it suited this land well, not Japan. Surrounded by the Chain Bridge, which gives the illusion of being crushed when you imagine its weight, and the magnificent buildings on the hills of Buda, this space may be the world of Bartok music itself.

Photo 104: Bartok Museum, which stands quietly on the hill of Buda

I sat in a cafe on the banks of the River Danube and listened to the Bartok cassette tape I had bought at the souvenir shop. This music, which I listened to in front of the Chain Bridge and the hills of Buda that shine in the setting sun, matched the atmosphere of this place. I was convinced that the great musician was produced by the land, and nodded sleepily in the mellow mood of a soothing Hungarian beer.

(3) Cityscape of Pest

The street extending east from the Chain Bridge leads to the City Park with Heroes' Square as the entrance. This is the main street of the city called the "People's Republic Street." It was also called "Andras Street" during the Austro-Hungarian Empire, "Road connecting 'Hitler Square' and 'Mussolini Square'" during the Nazi German era, and "Stalin Street" after World War II. In the bright morning sun, I decided to take a stroll down this street.

The buildings that face the street are beautifully unified to a height of about five stories and all quite old. Being alone on the street corner made me feel like I had gone back in time hundreds of years. However, the modern souvenir shop and cafeteria on the first floor of a building quickly caused my illusion to fade.

Photo 105: A fountain shining in the summer sun in the city of Pest

Photo 106: A corner in Pest city

There are two lanes on each side in the center of the road, and next to these are green areas with grass. On the other side of the green belt, there were one-lane roads. Therefore, if you walk in front of the buildings facing the street, you will not be bothered by the noise of cars. There were some roundabouts and the water droplets scattered from the fountains in the roundabouts were shining in the early autumn sunlight.

In addition to ordinary buses, there were trolley buses and tram networks in the city. As I walked down the street, these vehicles often passed by. The city is also the birthplace of the subway. At the end of the nineteenth century, the world's first electric train ran underground. The subway still passes under the River Danube to connect Buda and Pest.

After walking along the People's Republic Street for about 30 minutes, I discovered a large park at the end of the street. The entrance to the park was called Heroes' Square, where the equestrian statues of the Magyar tribe and the tall statues of successive Hungarian kings line up to look down on the square.

On both sides of the square were magnificent museums and galleries with thick marble columns facing each other. The interior of one museum was almost entirely made of marble and the large doors and the atrium where sunlight entered were beautifully demonstrated in the large space. The masterpieces of so-called European painting masters such as Raphael, Rembrandt, Rubens, Van Gogh, and Renoir were naturally displayed in harmony with the space.

Proceeding from Heroes' Square to the inside of the park, I was pleased to find a place of relaxation for the citizens. People enjoyed the late summer sunshine by strolling through the green groves and sunbathing shirtless. As I passed through the grove, I saw a sparkling spring pond. It was filled with clean water, and on the island in the pond, there was a castle that displayed

Photo 107: A spring pond and an old castle in Budapest City Park

the medieval architecture of Hungary. The Lotus leaves floated in the pond, the dark green aquatic plants swayed, and the water was clear and reflected the shadow of the castle, probably because there were few microorganisms. Here, the passage of time seemed slow.

Interestingly, there were hot springs in the park and several people were enjoying the hot spring pool. There were several other hot springs in the vicinity, many of which seemed to have been developed under the occupation of Türkiye in the 16th century. I heard that there were many Turkish-style steam baths. I never thought I would meet a Turkish bath in such a distant place.

After strolling around the public park, I found a chair on a small cafe terrace facing the street and had a meal of "Western cuisine": pizza and Coca-Cola. When I looked at the guidebook to find out where to go next, I found information about the Institute of Geography. Curious, I decided to go to explore a corner on the southeast side of the civic park. It was a calm corner housing the embassies and consulates of various countries. Finally, I found the Institute of Geography, an interesting building with three sharp roofs. It had a unique design by Lechner Eden, known as the Gaudi of Hungary. The combination of pale yellow walls and blue and brown edging was reminiscent of a fairy tale, and the fine wooden double doors had a traditional look. I was curious about what kind of research was being conducted there, but unfortunately there was no information available to me at the time. When I sneaked a peek into the open basement window, I could see a drawing board and photogrammetric equipment in a dimly lit room that looked like a Vermeer painting.

Looking up at the triangular roof of the building, there was a sculpture of a man carrying a globe on his back. This must have been the symbol of this institute. What was the view of the world that created "geography" in the middle of the continent, where people have been fiercely moving around since ancient times?

Photo 108: Hungarian Institute of Geography. A globe can be seen on the triangular roof.

(4) Asia in Hungary, Hungary in Europe

At the restaurant, a friendly waiter talked to me as I was drinking Hungarian specialty wine. First, we talked about each other's names. The waiter asked,

"Is Suzuki your first name?"

"No, it's a family name," I answered, remembering that I wrote my last name first when I filled out my Hungarian visa application. So I asked, "Do you use your family name first in Hungary?"

"Yes," he answered.

The format of the address on the visa application form was also in the order of country, prefecture, city, local district, and so on, and the date was written in the order of year, month, and day. It can be said that "looking at a narrow object after recognizing such a wide object" is a way of zooming in from the viewpoint from above. This is exactly the same idea as in Japan; in other words, it can be said to be "Asian style." In this sense, I have seen "Asia" in Hungary.

The people walking around the city have the appearance of Europeans and the art and culture there are especially influenced by Austria. Nevertheless, they may still have the consciousness and pride of Asian Magyar in their

Photo 109: Budapest East Station, the starting point for the journey to Vienna, with beautiful flowers hanging from the ceiling

hearts. Calling themselves Magyar, they proudly decorated the equestrian statues of their ancestors and carved the history of their prosperity into the stone. Unfortunately, it was not possible to know the extent of such awareness among the citizens during a short stay.

I've heard that blue-eyed parents sometimes give birth to black-eyed children and children with Mongolian spots (congenital benign birthmarks). Thus, even though the culture and lifestyle that appear on the surface are completely "European," "Asia" may still be alive in the fundamental ideas and blood.

A taxi driver once complained to me, "As you say, Budapest is a beautiful city, but the ideology of this country is not good." I was so surprised by the Western art, culture and cityscape of Budapest that I completely forgot that I was still in the "East." Hungary, like other Eastern European countries, has experienced many economic problems such as huge external debt, and was in the process of making major reforms such as the introduction of a multi-party system.

International trains to Vienna depart from the Budapest East Station. I boarded the train there. The train was the Orient Express from Bucharest via

Vienna and Munich to Paris. However, it was an old-fashioned train, dark in color, far from the image of its name.

When I entered the car, it was very crowded with passengers carrying large suitcases and other luggage. When I found a seat that was vacant for one person and sat down, I found myself next to a Romanian family who had come from Bucharest. They liked the Japanese- Romanian phrasebook I had, which triggered a conversation. The older gentleman spoke German, and eventually the conversation became a mixture of German and English. I felt like I shouldn't casually ask the purpose of their trip, but apparently they were going to stay in Vienna. Going to Austria should be a special experience for them as Romanians are severely restricted from traveling abroad. I was asked many times if I knew the price of a hotel in Vienna. The eyes were serious. I thought again that I was still in the "East."

The railroad that runs west alongside the River Danube leads to Austria. The construction of private houses seems to have become neat and solid due to the use of western building materials and construction techniques.

The border may divide everything, depending on the time and place, but sometimes it doesn't mean much at all. After crossing such a mysterious border, the world beyond will become completely "Europe."

CHAPTER 3
Beyond the turbulent end of the 20th century [2019]

When I wandered the Balkan Peninsula alone after spending the summer of 1988 in Türkiye, the destabilization of the Balkans had already begun due to the effects of the perestroika in the Soviet Union in 1985 and the Chernobyl nuclear power plant accident in 1986. However, I had not witnessed any concrete signs of such destabilization. In September 1989, the border between Hungary and Austria was opened. The Constitution of the Republic of Hungary was enacted that October, followed by the collapse of the Berlin Wall in November, and a peaceful transition of power occurred in Bulgaria. A revolution broke out in Romania in December, during which President Ceausescu and his wife Elena were executed.

Over 30 years have passed since the revolutions in Eastern Europe. Its social situation has transformed completely. There are no guards with rifles at the border station, and they no longer blow any warning whistles. Strict immigration checks have become a thing of the past. In retrospect, I am surprised that I was able to travel across the Balkan Peninsula alone on the eve of the revolution. I carried several phrasebooks with me because each country had a different language. Every time I crossed a border, the currency of the nation I was exiting became just another piece of paper. My travels presented a fruitful opportunity for me to contemplate the meaning of borders.

After arriving in Vienna, I crossed the Brenner Pass on the way from Innsbruck to Milan, from where I flew to Athens. From there, I returned to Japan with the ticket that I had stowed away at the bottom of my wallet. Thirty-one years later, I returned to Istanbul. Türkiye had undergone major changes since my last visit (Table 2). The Izmit-Kocaeli and Düzce earthquakes occurred in quick succession in 1999. Subsequently, the geopolitical landscape of Middle East became unstable. Prime Minister Erdogan became the President of Türkiye in 2014. Erdogan's authority was further consolidated after the failed coup d'état in 2016. I began to wonder how Istanbul—the eternal city—had changed and how my old friends there were doing.

Table2: Turkish chronology (since the 1980s)

1980	Coup d'etat by the Turkish Armed Forces
1982	New constitution enacted
	(1983.10.30 M6.9 Erzurum Earthquake)
	[1991 Gulf War]
	(1992.3.13 M6.7 Erzincan Earthquake)
	(1999.8.17 M7.6 Izmit Kocaeli Earthquake)
	(1999.11.12 M7.2 Duzce Earthquake)
2007	Constitutional amendment, Presidential referendum system
	(2011.10.23 M7.2 Van Earthquake)
2014	Prime Minister Erdogan became president.
2016	Attempted coup d'etat by a part of the Turkish Armed Forces killed 290 people.
2017	Constitutional amendment, Abolition of parliamentary cabinet system
	(2019.9.26 M5.8 Marmara Sea / Istanbul Earthquake)
	(2020.10.30 M7.0 Izmir Earthquake)

Photo 110: Attempted coup d'etat in Türkiye. People standing on Turkish tanks in Ankara (July 16, 2016, Reuters = Kyodo)

1. New Istanbul Airport

(1) Turkish moon

I landed at the Istanbul International Airport before dawn on September 15, 2019. The airport, which opened in October 2018, is located 35 km northwest of the city of Istanbul on the Black Sea Coast. Four runways had been completed, and two more runways are scheduled to be added to render it one of the busiest airports in Europe in terms of passenger traffic. The airport was sparsely populated before dawn, 5 am and its beautifully designed concourse was spacious. I finally arrived at the immigration counter after traversing several connecting escalators.

During my first visit to Istanbul in 1988, I arrived at Ataturk International Airport in downtown Istanbul. We arrived before dawn and were greeted by Prof. Işıkara near the immigration gate. Were able to enter the country without stringent immigration checks due to his help. The hustle and bustle outside the airport building amazed me. This time around, the immigration procedure proceeded smoothly. When I reached the large airport lobby, Mustafa welcomed me. His hair had turned silver, but his gentle smile was unchanged.

"*Merhaba! Nasılsınız*?" (Hello, how are you?)

Since he had studied in Japan in the early 1990s, he spoke in Japanese.

"*Oh, Genki-desuka*?" (Are you fine?)

He playfully extended his hands. I had emailed him before my departure and asked him to pick me up at around 7 a.m. because I was scheduled to arrive far too early in the morning. However, the Turkish gentleman did not want to keep his friend waiting.

Mustafa's car, Toyota Auris was parked at the new airport's spacious parking lot. We entered the car, left the airport, and made our way to the highway. The new highway continued to the city of Istanbul, where Mustafa lived.

A cool dawn breeze was blowing as I opened the window. The full moon was shining in the western sky. I remembered seeing the moon beyond a mosque's spire as I made my way through the city from Ataturk Airport back in 1988. On that day, the moon was a waning crescent in the eastern sky. The moon looks especially great here in Türkiye.

Photo 111: Early morning *adhan* echoes from the mosque in Bakırköy, Istanbul.

Upon turning the gentle curve at the exit of the highway, we entered the quiet neighborhood of Bakırköy. We eventually arrived at the six-story apartment building where Mustafa lived. The surrounding area was calm, and the street was lined with poplars and linden trees that had begun to change color. A small mosque with a spire stood on the opposite side of the road.

(2) Listening to the Adhan with Mustafa

Mustafa's home was on the 5th floor. There was a sofa near the entrance in the living room, and beautiful paintings and decorations were hung on the room's white walls.

"*Doh-zo*" (Please), Mustafa said in Japanese.

At 6 a.m., the mosque across the street commenced its adhan as the day dawned. The loud voice of the adhan echoing in this foreign city sounded like a welcome greeting to my ears. Mustafa turned to me and said, "Why don't you sleep for a while? My family is still sleeping." Then, he began checking emails on his laptop. I tried resting on the sofa, but I could not sleep as I was overwhelmed by the joy of being back there after such a long gap. The situation resembled the one when I first visited back in 1988. We crossed the Bosphorus Strait and stayed at the guesthouse at Boğaziçi University's Kandilli Observatory, which was located on a hill overlooking the strait. The bright red dahlia flowers placed on the table were impressive.

"How are all your Turkish friends?" I asked.

"They are doing fine. However, the situation differs for each person."

He then updated me about each of them.

"How about everyone in Japan? How about Mr. Ito?"

Mr. Ito is an uncle of mine who lives in Tokyo. Mustafa studied abroad at the Tokyo Institute of Technology for two years in the 1980s, during which he stayed at Ookayama. Turkish people were rare in Japan at that time, and it was extremely difficult for him to find a room to rent. On my behalf, my uncle walked around with Mustafa for days in search of a place for him to stay. He finally found him a room on the second floor of a wooden apartment and signed as his guarantor. My uncle had wandered around Europe for a year in the 1960s, when he was a university student. He said he helped Mustafa in order to pay forward the kindness of those who took care of him at the time. He is Mustafa's best benefactor in Japan, and Mustafa still loves him a lot.

"By the way, I'm glad that Mitsubishi withdrew from constructing the Sinop Nuclear Power Plant." I mentioned the news I read in the newspaper.

"Yeah, that was good," Mustafa replied.

As earthquake researchers, we were very concerned about the relationship between nuclear power plants and earthquakes. Sinop is a city on the Black Sea coast in northern Türkiye. There have been concerns about the city's safety owing to its proximity to the Anatolian Fault, which is a plate boundary that frequently experiences earthquakes. It has also been pointed out that there might be another active fault in the immediate vicinity of the city.

The relationship between nuclear power plants and active faults has attracted significant attention. I have been engaged in the preparation of guides for seismic examinations by the Nuclear Safety Commission since 2007. Additionally, I contributed to the establishment of the Nuclear Regulation Authority's (NRA) regulatory standards and the investigation of active faults at the site of nuclear power plants. My call for strong nuclear regulation at an NRA meeting was heavily reported on television. As a result, I have been severely criticized by power companies and the researchers who defend these companies. I could not recall whether I had mentioned this to Mustafa, but he seemed to be aware of it.

"Is Türkiye still planning to construct a nuclear power plant?" I asked.

"Some of my fellow Turkish researchers have been sent to a nuclear agency in Vienna." he replied.

According to a news report from February 2021, the construction of the Akkuyu nuclear power plant on the Mediterranean coast of southern Türkiye had begun with help from Russia.

"How has earthquake disaster prevention progressed in Türkiye since the Great Earthquake of 1999?" I asked.

"Turks heat up and cool down quite easily, so they soon forget about such things..."

After a while, Mustafa's nine-year-old son (Ali Kemal), his wife (Sema), and his wife's mother (Emine) came downstairs and we exchanged greetings.

"Let's please have a breakfast together," Sema said as she invited me to the table.

A nostalgic breakfast consisting of warm bread (*ekmek*), various cheeses, tomatoes, cucumbers, and a small glass of *çay* adorned the table.

Mustafa's home occupied the fifth and sixth floors of a concrete apartment building. The balcony could be accessed from the upper floor of the house. A refreshing breeze blew through the calm city of Istanbul, which had just witnessed a splendid sunrise.

Photo 112: Mustafa and his wife, Sema

(3) Galata Pier's bustle

"Let me show you to your hotel," said Mustafa.

I left the house with Mustafa. We boarded the Auris again and drove to Zeytinburnu tram station. He parked on the street in front of the station and rode the tram with me.

We took the T1 tram line, which was established in 1992. The tram itself was also relatively new. The tram window presented a splendid view of the city. As I looked out the window, I realized how much I had missed the city's atmosphere. Mustafa sensed my joy and smiled.

We eventually arrived at Laleli Universite station, located in the middle of the old city of Istanbul. We could see the Istanbul University building in front of us. Tonight's inn was the calm five-story hotel in front of the station.

"This is your university, isn't it?" I asked Mustafa.

"That's right, but it's different now..."

He said that Istanbul University was divided in 2018 as a result of a government policy. Additionally, three other traditional universities were also divided and 15 new universities were established.

Photo 113: Faculty of Letters at Istanbul University and Laleli Universite Station [2019]

After seeing me off, Mustafa returned home. I took the tram again by myself and headed to Sirkeci station. It was the terminal station of the Orient Express, where I set out on my trip to Eastern Europe 31 years ago.

I wanted to visit the station's platform to watch the Orient Express depart. However, once I entered the station, I realized that its atmosphere had changed. Although there were traces of the old platform, the station was now mostly underground. An escalator led to the underground station, which was no longer a terminal for the Orient Express. The information board revealed that a new railway line continued from the underground station to both the east and west as the Marmaray Line. This line was directly connected to Asia.

I exited the station building with the shocking realization that it was no longer the memorable terminal station that I once knew. I went down the slope to the north of the station, from where I could see the sea right in front of me. I had arrived at the port of Eminönü in the Bosphorus Strait. A refreshing breeze blew into the sea, over which I spotted several seagulls and dozens of medium-sized passenger ships. Back when I had first visited Istanbul, this was a booming harbor where many people would gather.

Photo 114: Golden Horn connecting to the Bosphorus Strait, Galata Bridge, and Istanbul New City Area [2019]

Photo 115: Tram running on Galata Bridge [2019]

I actively released the camera shutter as I approached the coastline. On my left was the Galata Bridge, which spans the Golden Horn. The balustrade was lined with restaurants, and the bridge looked the same as when I last saw it. However, a tram was now running on the bridge. The guidebook indicated that the bridge had been rebuilt to allow trams to pass through. The center of the bridge now had a tram station, where people could disembark and walk to either side of the bridge.

Photo 116: Men hanging a fishing line from the top of the Galata Bridge [2019]

The New City, which leads to Taksim Square, stood beyond the bridge. In reality, the New City is only called so owing to its relative novelty in comparison to the ancient Old City. Built in the 14th century, the Galata Tower still stood on the small hills of the New City. The setting sun tilted west and coated the landscape in its warm color. Several people continued to traverse the bridge under this sunlight, and many men hung fishing lines along the bridge. Having finally returned to Istanbul from the eastern tip of Asia, standing at the bridge brought back memories from my last visit.

2. The current Bosphorus Strait

(I) Under-strait tunnel

"I want to go to Çengelköy," I had told Mustafa on the way from the airport just after my arrival. Çengelköy is on the bank of the Bosphorus opposite to Istanbul. It is a small port town at the foot of the hill on which Kandilli Observatory is located. Back when I first visited, we stayed at the observatory and went to the town for dinner almost every night. We had to take the bridge over the strait or board a crossover to get there back then. However, we could get there faster now via the Marmaray Railway.

Mustafa and I decided to meet at the underground platform of Sirkeci Station at 9:30 am. Sirkeci Station was the terminal of the Orient Express until 2013, but it is now on the railroad that connects Europe and Asia. I took a long escalator down to the platform on the 9th basement floor, where I met Mustafa. We then boarded a train to the Asian side of the Marmaray Railway.

Marmaray runs through a tunnel under the Bosphorus. The undersea tunnel was built by the Taisei Corporation with JICA funding from Japan. The deepest part of the strait is 60 m below sea level. The submerging structure method was adopted in the fast-flowing strait. The blueprint for the cross-strait tunnel was already drawn in 1860 during the Ottoman-Turkish era. Therefore, at the ceremony to commemorate the tunnel's penetration in 2011, President Erdogan said he was delighted that the 150-year-old dream of the Turkish people had finally come true. The collaboration between Türkiye and Japan to construct the tunnel deepened their friendship.

The train ran at a high speed as soon as it left Sirkeci station. Five minutes later, it arrived at Üsküdar station on the opposite bank. After alighting from the train, we went up on a long escalator to enter the sunny city of Üsküdar. Thirty-one years ago, we had come here via a *dolmuş* (shared taxi) from Çengelköy with Ms. Oya. The city appeared to have had a strong Islamic atmosphere and exoticism to it at that time, but it now only appears to be a neat cityscape. Many old fine buildings are facing a square in front of the harbor.

Çengelköy is approximately four kilometers north of the strait. We took a medium-sized bus this time. Although I wanted to take a closer look at the nostalgic cityscape along the strait, I could only fleetingly glimpse at it from the bus window. Eventually, I saw the Strait No. 1 Bridge, which was

Photo 117: Bosphorus Strait No. 1 Bridge (July 15 Martyrs' Bridge; provided by PIXTA)

Photo 118: Bosphorus Strait seen from the Asian side [2019]

constructed with British assistance in 1973. The view looking up from under the bridge was spectacular.

When I first came here on July 1, 1988, this was the only bridge that connected Europe and Asia. Two days later, the second bridge (Fatih Sultan Mehmet Bridge) was completed 6 km north of it. It was built by Ishikawajima Harima Heavy Industries (currently IHI) and Mitsubishi Heavy Industries with official development assistance from Japan. The Strait No.1 Bridge is

Photo 119: Fish food *locanta* seen from the teahouse in Çengelköy [2019]

now called the "15 July Martyrs' Bridge." The new name is in remembrance of the civilians who resisted and were killed by the soldiers who blocked the bridge during the attempted coup d'état by the military in 2016.

A while into our journey, I spotted the Çengelköy cityscape. There were big trees on the side of the road, and shops were lined up under their shade. The popular and quiet cityscape remained as it was when I first visited. "It must have been around here," I said while walking. Just then, I saw a couple of trees that evoked a memory. One tree only had stumps, whereas the other had a lush foliage. I heard that one of them had recently collapsed during a storm. Under the big tree, there were two restaurants facing the wharf. This used to be the place where we would enjoy dinner every night.

(2) Climbing to the hill to reach Kandilli.

The sun shone brightly. I sat facing Mustafa at the outdoor table of the restaurant I once frequented and drank some *çay*.

"This is your nostalgia," Mustafa said.

"That's right," I replied.

Photo 120: Former Kureli Military School facing the Strait [2019]

"Then let's go to Kandilli," Mustafa said as he stood up.

"Would you like to go there by minibus?"

I preferred to walk during my nostalgic tours. Since this was the first foreign land I visited, I wanted to slowly explore in search of the remnants of my past. After heading north along the strait for a while, I saw the elegant building of Kuleli Military High School, which had a splendid pointed roof. Built in the mid-19th century, it was Türkiye's oldest military high school. However, it had been closed after the attempted coup d'état in 2016.

We climbed the long, winding slope adjacent to the school. We passed by an old private house and eventually arrived at Kandilli Observatory's guard post. Mustafa worked here until 2010, so he was acquainted with the guard and introduced me to him in Turkish. He told the guard that I was visiting for the first time in 30 years. The guard smilingly said "*Hoş geldiniz!*" (Welcome) and let me in.

The slope continued on straight from the guard post. There was a new dormitory in the square where the children once played soccer, but everything else had largely stayed the same. Poplar trees swayed in the wind on the side

Photo 121: Tree-lined road leading to Kandilli Observatory [2019]

of the road, the scent of fig trees drifted with the breeze, and pine trees grew on the mountain's gentle slopes.

We finally reached Kandilli Observatory after a tiresome uphill walk. Same as before, the observatory contained sparsely built two-story offices and research buildings with bright brick-colored roofs—typical of the Mediterranean region—along narrow winding roads.

"This is the building where I worked," Mustafa said as he showed me around the old building.

"That is Professor Işıkara's office"

When I entered there, the names of Professors Işıkara and Balamir, who once took care of me, were listed on the door of the room labeled "Memorial."

"Do you remember this house?" Mustafa asked.

"Oh yes, that's the guest house we stayed in."

It looked the same as it did back when I first visited. Since the Turks had a humorous disposition, they named the two guest houses at the observatory the "Snake House" and the "Mosquito House," respectively. In front of the Snake House, a pale pink oleander was in full bloom, just as it was back then.

(3) Professor Işıkara!

As I walked further, I came across an unfamiliar new building. Curiously, I was drawn to it. I found out that it was the disaster prevention education building, which was built after the Izmit-Kocaeli earthquake in 1999 and was fabricated using Japanese research funds. The door of the exhibition

Photo 122: Geophysics Research Building at Kandilli Observatory [2019]

Photo 123: Nameplate of the research building [2019]

room was closed. I peeked inside through the clear glass and spotted exhibits that explained the mechanism of the earthquake, models that outlined the earthquake resistance mechanism of the building, and explanation panels for fixing furniture. When I went to the hall beside the exhibition room, there were five or six portraits hanging on the wall. One of them was nostalgic.

"Professor Işıkara!" I exclaimed.

Professor Işıkara was a big source of encouragement during my visit 31 years ago. He offered his support as I headed into Eastern Europe alone after the investigation by saying, "If you ever have any problems, please contact me from anywhere." The portraits thus helped me realize why I was attracted to this building.

On the way back from Kandilli, we noticed a wagon that was parked in front of the main building, beside the main gate.

"That was Professor Işıkara's exclusive car. Since the number plate has 'DD' on it, it was fondly called *Deprem Dede's* (earthquake grandfather's) car," Mustafa explained.

After the Izmit-Kocaeli earthquake, Professor Işıkara made regular TV appearances to explain the importance of earthquake disaster prevention. As a result, the citizens gave him this nickname.

3. 20 years after the Izmit-Kocaeli earthquake

(1) Highway on Marmara coast.

Mustafa and I met early in the morning at Zeytinburnu Station of the T1 tram and drove to Izmit in Kocaeli Province, which was the epicenter of the earthquake in 1999. Our Auris zipped through the city and arrived on the Asian side through the Bosphorus tunnel. Mustafa conversed with his friend Şerif over the phone as he drove.

After a while, we spotted Şerif standing on the side of the highway. Şerif lived near the strait and was a professor at the University of Kocaeli. It had been a long time since I last met Şerif in Türkiye. He certainly looked older, but his easygoing nature remained the same. When I was conducting the survey in 1988, he was preparing to study abroad in Japan.

He told me about the earthquake in 1999. The University of Kocaeli was located at the center of the epicentral area. According to Mustafa, Şerif gained some fame through the regular TV appearances he made to provide details regarding the earthquake.

"You made a lot of money, didn't you?" said Mustafa.

"Oh yeah, that's how I built my house," Şerif retorted jokingly.

Şerif also conducted international collaborative research. He played an important role in a big project, but he said he was not convinced by the policy of the project and thus turned down its related position. They value their own principles and do not interfere with the way of life of others.

When I inquired about Türkiye's relationship with Japan after the Izmit-Kocaeli earthquake, both Şerif and Mustafa responded positively. They have still good relations with Japanese colleagues in some joint projects. However, I think that, from my experience in other countries, Japanese research funds have limited uses and have not contributed to important aspects such as human resource development at observatories. International research cooperation cannot function effectively unless researchers in the country being supported are provided discretionary power over the execution of the budget.

Şerif continues to raise awareness regarding earthquake prevention on the radio. On the other hand, Mustafa's approach to disaster prevention involves mainly providing support for relevant scientific basic research.

(2) Izmit-Kocaeli Earthquake

Owing to the lack of traffic on the highway, we reached Kocaeli within two hours. During the 1988 survey, our research team took several minibuses from Kandilli to get to Kocaeli. We tied our suitcases and research equipment on the roofs of the buses with ropes and drove along the ordinary road facing Izmit Bay in the Sea of Marmara.

This area on the northern coast of the Sea of Marmara was the center of the affected area in 1999. Professor Barka of Istanbul Technical University, who was with us during our joint research, published the following report in *Science* (A. Barka, 1999, *Science*, 285, 1858–1859). The contents are summarized as follows.

Photo 124: Izmit-Kocaeli Earthquake (August 1999, Reuters = Kyodo)

Photo 125: Gölcük (August 1999, Kyodo News), where the restaurant area was submerged due to the subsidence caused by faulting

The Mw 7.4 Izmit-Kocaeli Earthquake occurred at 3:02 a.m. on August 17, 1999. The focal depth was approximately 10–16 km and strong shaking lasted for 37 seconds. The greatest damage was caused to Izmit, at the eastern end of the Sea of Marmara , close to the epicenter, while considerable damage also occurred in Istanbul, approximately 70 km away. Phone lines were cut off, roads were flooded with residents, entire buildings were destroyed, and many people were killed. A fire broke out in the oil refineries along the Gulf of Izmit and burned for 5.5 days. The naval base and shipyard at Gölcük was cut at the surface by a 4-m strike-slip fault and at least 400 military personnel were killed. The number of deaths and missing persons across the area reached 17,000.

The fault continued 90 km east–west from Gölcük in the west and through Izmit, Sapanca, and Akyazı to Gölyaka in the east. Maximum displacement occurred along the surface fault east of Sapanca, where the road was offset right-laterally by 5 m . In Gölcük, the ground was subsided over 100 m along the fault, causing hotels and shops to sink .

The Izmit-Kocaeli Earthquake was the seventh in a series of earthquakes that have continued to move west since 1939 along the 100-km-long North Anatolian Fault and its occurrence in 1999 increased the risk of earthquakes west of Gölcük and Istanbul. The preceding 1719 and 1754 earthquakes killed 6,000 and 2,000 people, respectively in the area between Istanbul and Adapazarı, while the 1878 earthquake caused great damage to the eastern part of the Sea of Marmara, in the Sapanca and Adapazarı regions, and the 1894 earthquake killed 1,400 people along the coast.

The location of the 1999 Izmit earthquake was similar to that of the 1719 earthquake. According to GPS measurements, the deep North Anatolian Fault is steadily displaced by –15 mm/year. Such deep displacement can cause an intermittent displacement of 4–5 m at the surface every 300 years. Therefore, "the location and severity of this earthquake should not have come as a surprise" (Balka, 1999).

Professor Barka was a soft-spoken person. I still remember him driving around in his Renault. I wondered why he used the term "not have come as a surprise" in his report about the earthquake. He may have wanted to convey that the occurrence of the earthquake was natural and inevitable. Furthermore, according to the paper he wrote in 2002 (Barka et al., 2002, *Bulletin of the Seismological Society of America*, 92, 43–60), earthquakes have regularly occurred in the region over the last 300 years (Fig. 16). Earthquakes struck the northern part of the Sea of Marmara in 1719, 1754, and 1766. There were more earthquakes in 1878 and 1894 as well. The 1999 earthquake struck the area to the west of the epicenter of the 1966 earthquake. The active fault on the seafloor of the Sea of Marmara off the coast of Istanbul is of great concern. However, no major earthquake has occurred on this fault since 1766.

(3) Remnant surface earthquake faults

Şerif guided us through traces of surface faults that still remained. Twenty years later, the embankment of the stream that flowed through a residential area in the suburbs of Izmit was still off to the right by a few meters. At the time of the earthquake, the five-story building near here was destroyed. He also said that he did not know if the cause of the building's collapse was the frequency of the earthquake viblation or the extension of the penthouse on the sixth floor. Although it is difficult to identify remnants of the earthquake now, many people undoubtedly suffered back when the earthquake occurred.

Kocaeli University is located on a hill north of Izmit. On the way there, I saw houses that were reconstructed after the earthquake. These were well-built condominiums, which indicated to me that a lot of money was invested into the post-earthquake reconstruction. I learned that during the Ottoman period, Türkiye compensated those who were affected by earthquakes. Although this is beneficial for the victims, some Japanese researchers have

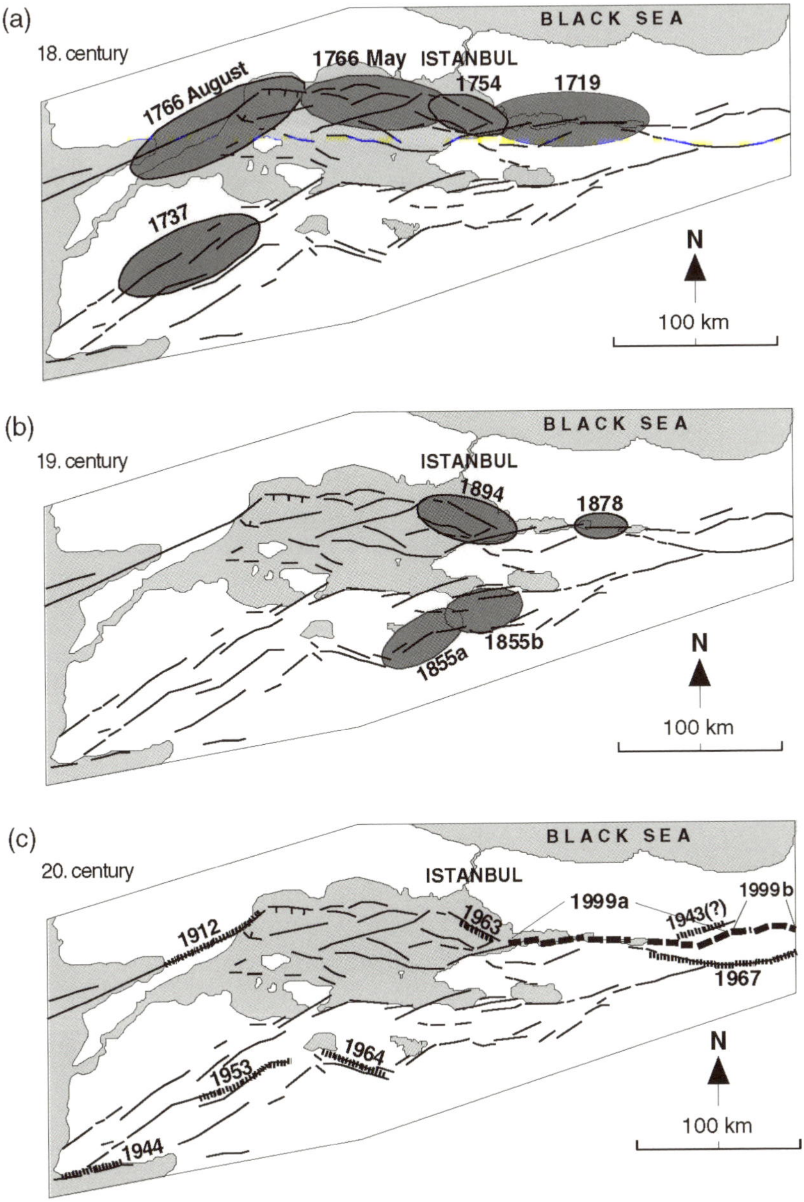

Fig. 16: Distribution map of historical earthquakes near Istanbul (Barka et al., 2002, *Bulletin of the Seismological Society of America*, 92)

indicated that the provision of excessive compensation can lead citizens to neglect disaster prevention practices.

Photo 126: Lateral displacement of river embankment remains to the east of Izmit Bay [2019]

Our 1988 survey site was based on Iznik, 40 km southwest of Izmit. I heard that the town of Akyazı, where I had been with Dr. Ikeda and Vuslat for 10 days for a trench survey, was damaged the most. The dormitory of the forestry office, where we stayed back then, may have collapsed. I wanted to go there, but I unfortunately could not.

(4) Development of the seismic observation network

Kocaeli University is a national university with 60,000 students. Şerif led a seismology course there with several young researchers. When we visited there, a TV station crew were reporting on the new observation network around Bursa that Şerif and his colleagues were developing. When Şerif mentioned to the crew that a Japanese researcher was visiting, they requested to interview me. They asked me why Japan chose to engage in the joint research project with Türkiye. I mentioned that both Japan and

Türkiye are earthquake-prone countries that hope to mitigate the damage caused by such disasters. Additionally, I indicated that many researchers from both countries share a friendly bond and have conducted collaborative research since the 1970s.

I frequently worry about the potentially large earthquakes that may strike Istanbul in the future. Professor Barka's paper also highlighted that the risk of earthquakes around Istanbul is increasing. The 1999 earthquake occurred along the North Anatolian fault. This fault extends further west on the bottom of the Sea of Marmara, just south of Istanbul. If an earthquake occurs there, the city of Istanbul will inevitably be damaged.

In the eighteenth century, Istanbul suffered particularly great damage. Istanbul's population has grown rapidly. It was less than one million in 1950, but increased to seven million as of 1990 and is currently over seventeen million. The population primarily burgeoned due to the influx of settlers from the Anatolia region and increase in the birth rate. In addition, migrants from the Balkan Peninsula and refugees from the Middle East also added to the population.

An earthquake in the region could result in unfathomable damage and the collapse of several structures. Mustafa told us about the current state of earthquake countermeasures in Türkiye. The rebuilding of schools and hospitals began the year after the earthquake. Seismic isolation is now required for new hospital buildings. Viaducts and major bridges were also reinforced. The disaster prevention city plan commenced in 2014, and all cities were required to formulate and complete a damage mitigation plan by September 2021.

A new seismic standard was established in 2018 and was enacted on January 1, 2019. The owners of vulnerable buildings were provided with low interest rate loans, up to four years of rent subsidies, and property tax relief in order to facilitate a rebuild. Four years of disaster prevention education has become compulsory in elementary schools, and a vocational school and university department related to crisis management and disaster prevention measures have also been established.

Istanbul was damaged by the 1766 earthquake (magnitude 7.1) and the 1894 earthquake (magnitude 7.0). The death toll was approximately 4,000 for the former and 1,300 for the latter. The epicenters were on the North Anatolian Fault, which runs through the Sea of Marmara.

After my return to Japan, a magnitude 5.7 earthquake struck about 30 km off the Sea of Marmara on September 26, 2019, at 1:59 p.m.. No one died, but a mosque's spire collapsed, some buildings cracked, and many students and residents were evacuated to the streets. I heard that the university campus where Mustafa worked was severely damaged because it was located near the Marmara coast. Therefore, the campus moved to inland city 7 km north by the end of the year.

The towering appearance of the Sultan Ahmet Mosque (Blue Mosque) and Hagia Sophia, which have experienced several major earthquakes and have been restored each time, display the resilience of Türkiye. Although this assuages my worry, I cannot help but hope that this city where my friends live does not get hit by another major earthquake.

4. On the changing street corner of Istanbul

(1) Tram in the historical city.

A particularly major change in Istanbul over the last 30 years was the introduction of trams. The T1 line, which runs in the middle of the old historical city, was opened in 1992. The T4 line that extends north from the city center was opened in 2007. Lastly, the T5 line was launched in 2021. In addition, the nostalgic revival of the 19th century tram (T2: revived in 1990; T3: built in 2003) and six subway lines (M1: 1989; M2: 2000; M3: 2013; M4: 2012; M5: 2015; M6: 2015) were completed. Six subway lines are presently under construction and will eventually connect to the Istanbul New Airport.

The T1 tram is a masterpiece. Trams occupy the middle of a winding old cobblestone road in the heart of the old city, where the Hagia Sophia, the Sultan Ahmet Mosque, and the Grand Bazaar are located. Roads often turn at right angles, and the five- to six-car trams are designed execute such turns at high speeds. The pedestrians on the sidewalk get nervous when the trams blow past them. The cars also refrain from driving close to the tram tracks. Japan believes that the revival of trams that once ran in major cities is impossible, but is that notion correct? If you look at the T1 tram, you can clearly understand that such a revival is possible.

According to Mustafa, there was also opposition to the construction of trams in Istanbul. However, due to the city's rapid urbanization, measures against traffic problems (especially traffic congestion in the city center) became integral. Additionally, combatting air pollution and reducing carbon dioxide emissions and fossil fuel consumption became necessary. Despite the introduction of various tram and subway lines, they are still believed to be

Photo 127: T1 Tram running in front of Hagia Sophia [2019]

in short supply.

As I took the tram from Sultan Ahmet Station, I was soon exposed to Turkish compassion. A seemingly sick woman was staggering in the crowded tram car. The passengers around her noticed this and offered her support. The people around her called out to the driver, who opened the closed tram door. Microphones may be kindly installed in each tram car so that passengers' voices reach the driver. Then, several passengers got off with her and made her sit on the bench at the station. Witnessing this incident impressed me tremendously, as it demonstrated that Turkish people never overlook the plight of others. Such displays of collective solidarity are what makes a city thrive.

(2) Istanbul University area

The Grand Bazaar is like a maze. Created in the 15th century as per the Sultan's orders, it prospered as a caravan market on the Silk Road. It was damaged by the 1894 earthquake but was later repaired. The bazaar has 20 entrances and one can get lost in it quite easily. Owing to the frequent terror attacks in the country several years ago, a metal detection gate has been installed at every entrance.

Photo 128: Metal detector installed at the entrance of the Grand Bazaar [2019]

The number of pullers-in at shops seemingly decreased in comparison to 31 years ago. The dim bazaar boasted of several small shops that sold carpets, lamps, pottery, spices, and clothing. I informed Mustafa that I wanted to buy a rug. He took me to a small antique shop that was run by his classmate at Istanbul University. When I sat down there, the owner served me some *çay*. After talking about old tales for a while, Mustafa said, "Well then, let's go."

The manager of the antique shop took me to a carpet shop at the back of the bazaar. The Turks have a saying that goes "The friends of my friend are my important friends." The carpet store owner spread out rugs of varying patterns and colors one after another and elucidated meanings of the tradi-

Photo 129: Lamp shop in the Grand Bazaar [2019]

Photo 130: Magnificent Istanbul University main gate [2019]

tional patterns that he displayed. The antique shop owner said, "It's all good and the prices are also reasonable." I decided to buy a rustic handmade carpet.

A street full of bookstores was located near the Grand Bazaar. It resembled the arcades and the second-hand bookstores in Tokyo. I could see books on topics such as geography, mathematics, and grammar inside the stores there. After passing through the small gate at the end of the street, we arrived at Istanbul University's main gate.

Photo 131: Beyazit Tower at Istanbul University [2019], built as a fire lookout tower by order of King Mahmut II in 1828

The main marble gate of Istanbul University bears an engraving that reads "Founded in 1453." I entered the premises with Mustafa, who had graduated from the university and subsequently became a professor there. A garden lined with trees and a magnificent building were present at the back of the path. Bronze statues also graced the premises. The cylindrical building in the garden is used for astronomical observations. It looked like a ruin in the early modern period. There was a restaurant for professors next to the main gate. A chandelier reminiscent of one in a palace was hung in the restaurant, where faculty members and students quietly enjoyed lunch.

(3) *Locanta* in front of the Suleymaniye mosque

We entered the Istanbul University campus from the south-facing main gate and exited from the west gate. We then reached a quaint place, which also happened to be a World Heritage Site. A large Süleymaniye mosque stood there.

We entered a small restaurant (*lokanta*) that was near the mosque's gate. Half of the seats in the *lokanta* were placed outdoors. It resembled the "*udon*" or "*oden*" shops near Japanese temples. We ordered traditional Turkish eggplant stuffed with meat (*dolma*), stewed white beans, and *ayran* (salt yogurt drink).

Photo 132: Mustafa and author in a *locanta* in front of Suleymaniye Mosque [2019]

Here, we discussed the recent condition of universities in both countries. Mustafa complained about how the University of Istanbul was divided into several parts and his faculty was subsequently moved to another university: Istanbul University–Cerrahpaşa. Some of the traditional universities were suddenly converted into new universities due to a governmental policy.

I asked him about his friends once again. He told me that everyone still worked at the Kandilli Observatory at Boğaziçi University when earthquake struck in 1999. Later, Ali became a professor at Boğaziçi University and Şerif began to teach at Kocaeli University. Oya became a professor at Kocaeli University and later retired. She is now a marathon runner. Naz married a Dutch researcher, resigned and went to Netherland with her husband. Nurcan became the Director of Comprehensive Nuclear-Test-Ban Treaty

Organization in Vienna. Vuslat landed a job with a Japanese company. I would love to meet them all soon.

(4) The Adhan's big chorus

After Mustafa returned to the university for work, I visited the Sultan Ahmet Mosque (Blue Mosque) and Hagia Sophia alone. Muslims still prayed at the Blue Mosque, which was built in the early 17th century. This mosque and Hagia Sophia face each other across a large square. The Hagia Sophia was as a Christian, Greek Orthodox church in the Byzantine Empire in the 4th century, but was converted into a mosque by Ottoman Türkiye in 1453. After losing World War I, Türkiye was divided by the Western powers. Türkiye eventually achieved independence in 1934, and the Hagia Sophia was turned into a museum the following year.

The Hagia Sophia receives tourists from many countries now. There were more Koreans and Chinese people there than Japanese people. The mural on its ceiling depicted a Christian icon. The museum also had an Islamic prayer table on display. Major renovation work was also underway to ensure the preservation of the exhibits.

Photo 133: Hagia Sophia [2019]

Photo 134: Mural of Christ [2019]

Photo 135: Interior view of Hagia Sophia [2019]

I was impressed by the marble pattern on the floor. How many people have stepped on this before the marble has been so polished. This reminded me of the phrase, "Geography is the study of elucidating the patterns of the earth, just as the patterns of jewels are polished and stand out."

EPILOGUE

"The Turkish people came out of the Mongolian plateau and settle in the west. The Japanese went to the east end. That's why we are brothers," said an old Turk. I still remember his friendly smile. It should be interesting if the commonality of roots is the basis of friendly feelings besides the influence of education. Neighboring countries are prone to problems; however, it may in a sense be easier to maintain friendly relations if there is a certain distance between nations.

My encounter with Türkiye in my twenties had a great impact on me. Being interested in geography, I visited a foreign country for the first time and was fascinated by the Bosphorus, the cityscape of Istanbul, and the climate of Anatolia. I was happy to get to know the people of the country and share a good time. I was also confident that I could build friendly relations with people from any country. I visited China in 1992, South Korea in 1993, Sakhalin in 1995, and Taiwan in 1999 for several years each for active fault research. It was actually from the Turkish survey that I acquired this research theme.

Recently, I have been to Mongolia frequently because Mongolia is also an earthquake-prone country. In the first half of the 20th century, there were a series of magnitude 8 earthquakes in western Mongolia. In 2018, we discovered a large active fault near Ulaanbaatar and are currently conducting joint research with Mongolians.

Japanese famous novelist, Mr. Ryotaro Shiba wrote in his work that Mongolians often say, "Turks went out of here and went to the western end" or "We are Japanese ancestors." Certainly, I sometimes feel the same roots as Japanese people in the features of Mongolians. In Mongolia, *orkhon* inscriptions written in Old Turkish in the 6th and 8th centuries have been discovered and it has been confirmed that the Turkish roots are also there. In the future I would like to create an opportunity for researchers from these three countries to gather in Mongolia, which is located between Japan and Türkiye, to commence joint research on disaster risk reduction.

Now that I have reached my 60th birthday, I am grateful for my encounter with Türkiye when I was young and would like to thank the many people who have supported me. Dr. Mustafa Kemal Tuncer kindly and carefully checked the manuscript in English. Mr. Hisashi Hashimoto, President of Kokon Shoin, kindly published my first essay in the monthly magazine "Geography" in 1989. Mr. Nobuo Sekita and Hideaki Seki carefully edited my manuscript at that time. Keigo Hayashi of Fubaisha edited the manuscript for the publication of the Japanese version book in 2021. Ms. Yumi Itabashi of Hachidori Inc. supported me to publish the English version in 2022. Dr. Yoshimori Honkura, Dr. Yasutaka Ikeda, and many other professors gave me an opportunity to conduct joint investigations in Türkiye. My family and relatives have supported my many years of research. Finally, I would like to thank all my friends from both Japan and Türkiye for their heartwarming friendship.